JOURNAL OF AMERICAN INDIAN EDUCATION

Volume 61, Number 1
Spring 2022

The *Journal of American Indian Education* (ISSN 0021-8731) is published three times a year in spring, summer, and fall by the University of Minnesota Press, 111 Third Avenue South, Suite 290, Minneapolis, MN 55401-2520. http://www.upress.umn.edu

Postmaster: Send address changes to *JAIE*, University of Minnesota Press, 111 Third Avenue South, Suite 290, Minneapolis, MN 55401-2520.

Inquiries about manuscript submissions should be sent to jaie@asu.edu. Further information about manuscript submission is in the back of this issue and available online at https://jaie.asu.edu/content/submit-manuscript.

Address subscription orders, changes of address, and business correspondence (including requests for permission and advertising orders) to *JAIE*, University of Minnesota Press, 111 Third Avenue South, Suite 290, Minneapolis, MN 55401-2520.

Subscriptions: Regular U.S. rates: individuals, 1 year (three issues) $38; libraries, 1 year $87. Other countries add $5 for each year's subscription. Checks should be made payable to the University of Minnesota Press. Back issues published after 2014: $21.50 for individuals and $32.50 for libraries (plus $6 shipping for the first copy, $1.25 for each additional copy inside the United States; $9.50 shipping for the first copy, $6 for each additional copy outside the United States). Back issues published before 2015: Please contact jaie@asu.edu.

Digital institutional subscriptions to the *Journal of American Indian Education* are available online through the Project MUSE Hosted Journals Program at https://muse.jhu.edu/.

Ananda M. Marin (Choctaw descent)
University of California, Los Angeles

Nathan Martin
Arizona State University

Stephen May
University of Auckland

Douglas L. Medin
Northwestern University

Robin Zape-tah-hol-ah Minthorn
(Kiowa/Apache/Nez Perce/Umatilla/
Assiniboine)
University of Washington

Sharon Nelson-Barber
(Rappahannock)
WestEd

Sheilah Nicholas (Hopi)
University of Arizona

Leonie Pihama (Māori)
University of Waikato

Jon Reyhner
Northern Arizona University

Monty Roessel (Diné)
Diné College

Mary Eunice Romero-Little (Cochiti)
Arizona State University

Graham Smith (Māori)
Te Whare Wananga o Awanuiarangi

Linda Tuhiwai Smith (Māori)
University of Waikato

Elizabeth Sumida Huaman
(Wanka/Quechua)
University of Minnesota

Amanda R. Tachine (Diné)
Arizona State University

Malia Villegas (Alutiiq/Sugpiaq)
Afognak Native Corporation

Stephanie Waterman (Onondaga)
University of Toronto

Leisy T. Wyman
University of Arizona

VOLUME 61, NUMBER 1,
SPRING 2022

Editors' Introduction

THE *JOURNAL OF AMERICAN INDIAN EDUCATION* has entered its 61st volume year! We are excited by the possibilities that lie ahead, beginning with the lineup of authors and articles in this issue.

We launch the volume with Vincent Werito and Vangee Nez, who ask us to consider the ways that Indigenous teachers think about their teaching practices and their students' learning practices when engaged through culturally appropriate materials. Their article, "'Light a Little Candle in Their Hearts': Learning From Educators of Indigenous Youth About Culturally Sustaining/Revitalizing Teaching Practices in Contemporary Contexts," raises important questions about what kinds of academic content matter and how Indigenous-based content should be used to teach Indigenous children. Werito and Nez ask us to consider Indigenous pedagogies and call for researchers to be more systematic and purposeful in focusing on Indigenous students who learn through Indigenous-centered pedagogies. In many ways, this article lays important groundwork for future research on the full meaning of pedagogy: the process of thinking about both teaching and learning.

In the next article, "'You're Not Going to Round Me to Zero, You're Going to Round Me to at Least One, I Will at Least Be One': Lumbee Erasure, Identity, and Stories of a Lumbee Professor and a Lumbee Student," Brittany Danielle Hunt and Megan Locklear raise the following questions: What does it mean to have a professor/teacher who understands your identity and your lived experiences? What does it mean to have a student who understands their professor's identity and lived experiences? Many Indigenous students still have not had an Indigenous professor. This article illuminates the need for the presence and visibility of teachers who understand their students and the power of those teachers in the learning of students.

And finally, Adam T. Murry, Tyara Marchand, Emily Wang, and Daniel Voth, in their article, "The Five-Factor Model of Indigenous Studies: A Quantitative Content Analysis of Postsecondary Indigenous Studies Websites in Canada, the United States, Australia, and New Zealand," offer four areas of intersection in Indigenous Studies programs in four countries. These global intersections, drawn from an analysis of websites, include Indigenous methodologies, Indigenous community involvement, Indigenous ways of knowing and being, and student communities. Their article inspires further questions for all of us: What role does Indigenous Studies play in service to our communities? What role *can* it play? What role *should* it play? The article is an invitation for deeper consideration of these questions.

Taken together, this trio of articles points us toward how language, culture, representation, and well-being intersect in learning communities, and their significance. These communities are dyads (Hunt and Locklear), teachers and youth (Werito and Nez), and higher education programming (Murry et al.). We agree that seeing oneself in the learning materials and teaching practices, and in the context of our own critically reflexive teaching, is crucial to vital Indigenous futures. We admire this collection of important research and are honored to bring it forward. Please enjoy, and gift this wisdom forward.

Warmly,

Bryan McKinley Jones Brayboy and Teresa L. McCarty,
Editors
Angelina E. Castagno and Patricia D. Quijada Cerecer,
Associate Editors

"Light a Little Candle in Their Hearts": Learning From Educators of Indigenous Youth About Culturally Sustaining/Revitalizing Teaching Practices in Contemporary Contexts

VINCENT WERITO AND VANGEE NEZ

Educators of Indigenous youth provide important insights about teaching Indigenous youth in contemporary educational contexts. Yet their perspectives about what constitutes effective pedagogical practices are often underappreciated. This qualitative study explores the different ways that nine educators of Indigenous youth constructed their pedagogical practice based on key features of Indigenous education and their cultural strengths. Three themes emerged from the study that reinforce the significance of (1) Indigenous content knowledge integration in school curriculum, (2) student and teacher relationships, and (3) educators' reflective thinking. The implications of this study for teacher education highlight the need for all educators to be conscious of what constitutes culturally revitalizing/sustaining pedagogy from the perspectives of Indigenous educators. Finally, the findings point to the need for more research on teaching Indigenous youth using Indigenous-centered pedagogy for contemporary practice.

Introduction

Early attempts to educate Native American (American Indian)[1] youth in the late 1800s were premised on an American colonial enterprise of "deculturalization" of dominated groups like Native Americans (Spring, 2007, p. 7). In particular, the idea of "American Indian education" (AIE) was created by American ideologies of "colonial education" (Lomawaima & McCarty, 2006) that were imposed upon American Indian/Indigenous communities. Prior to this time, Indigenous-centered pedagogies were key to transmitting community life skills through a lifelong search of knowledge for life's sake (Cajete, 1994). Indigenous-centered pedagogies are based upon an Indigenous worldview (i.e., epistemology, axiology, and philosophy) and informed by community cultural core values of respect, reciprocity, relationships, and responsibility (Cajete, 1999; Kawagley, 1995).

Starting in the mid-1960s, the goals of AIE have changed to include more conscious efforts by Indigenous communities to create Indigenous tribally controlled schools (Ah Nee-Benham, 2017; Lomawaima & McCarty, 2006). More recently Indigenous communities are including their traditional perspectives about teaching and learning (i.e., pedagogy) to perpetuate community cultural knowledge and languages through the medium of culturally responsive, community-based schooling (Battiste, 2013; Castagno & Brayboy, 2008; McCarty & Lee, 2015). Within the last 30 years there has been a gradual shift toward culturally relevant, responsive, and sustaining approaches to education, particularly for youth of color (Paris, 2012; Paris & Alim, 2017). Critical educational researchers (Gay, 2000; Ladson-Billings, 2009; Paris, 2012) have offered approaches to meet the diverse cultural and linguistic needs of students of color. For example, Paris (2012) defines culturally sustaining pedagogies (CSP) as seeking "to perpetuate and foster—to sustain—linguistic, literate, and cultural pluralism as part of the democratic project of schooling" (p. 95). Paris argues that CSP must do more and must be an extension of culturally responsive pedagogy such that the traditional and contemporary life experiences of students are sustained and used in teaching practices in the frame of Western (colonial) projects of schooling. Furthermore, he writes, "we must be open to sustaining them in both the traditional and evolving ways they are lived and used by contemporary young people" (p. 95).

Obviously, there are implications for looking at what these approaches may mean for different cultural groups, and in particular for sovereign Indigenous nations. For example, McCarty and Lee (2014) propose critical culturally sustaining/revitalizing pedagogy (CSRP) as "designed to address the socio-historical and contemporary contexts of Native American schooling" (p. 103). CSRP consists of three components that address the legacies of colonization, self-determination, and community-based accountability approaches. Incidentally, CSRP approaches can provide insights about what constitutes effective pedagogies for educating Indigenous youth in contemporary educational contexts based on the perspectives of educators who work with Indigenous youth.

The present study explores how educators of Indigenous youth construct pedagogical knowledge learned from teacher education programs as well as their own cultural backgrounds. The study underscores educators' critical reflections about what constitutes exemplary practices in AIE using a culturally revitalizing/sustaining pedagogical approach. Finally, the study highlights significant issues that underscore positive teacher dispositions (intellectual and social) that are needed for teaching youth of color in contemporary contexts.

Literature Review

A review of educational research in AIE reveals five key features of Indigenous (American Indian) education. These features include (1) acknowledging the legacies and/or remnants of oppression in education, (2) developing and implementing culturally relevant curriculum, (3) practicing culturally responsive schooling, (4) promoting the integration of Western constructs of knowledge into Indigenous knowledge systems, and (5) affirming student and teacher interactions (Bergstrom, Miller Cleary, & Peacock, 2003; Cajete, 1994; Kawagley, 1995; Klug & Whitfield, 2003; Lipka Mohatt, & the Ciulistet Group, 1998; Miller Cleary & Peacock, 1998). Taken together, these features of AIE describe significant culturally responsive schooling practices leading to positive outcomes for Indigenous youth (Castagno & Brayboy, 2008; Demmert, 2001).

First, acknowledging the legacies and/or remnants of oppression in AIE involves a critical examination of capitalism, patriarchy, settler-colonialism, and white supremacy that perpetuate the marginalization, racialization, and subjugation of Indigenous people and their knowledge systems (Haynes Writer, 2012; Klug & Whitfield, 2003; Lomawaima & McCarty, 2006; Miller Cleary & Peacock, 1998). Further, these critical examinations help reveal the present-day impacts of oppression on Indigenous urban and rural/tribal communities (Klug & Whitfield, 2003; Martinez, 2010; Miller Cleary & Peacock, 1998). However, the acknowledgment must move beyond despair and victimhood to highlight the cultural/tribal strengths and promise of Indigenous educational models (Battiste, 2013; Grande, 2004).

The second and third related features of AIE include creating culturally relevant curriculum and implementing culturally responsive pedagogical practices for Indigenous youth. Essentially, these combined features resonate with CSRP by integrating Indigenous ways of knowing into the everyday learning experiences of Indigenous youth (Bergstrom et al., 2003; Cajete, 1994; Castagno & Brayboy, 2008; Demmert, 2001; Kawagley, 1995; Klug & Whitfield, 2003; Lipka et al., 1998; Miller Cleary & Peacock, 1998). For example, Castagno and Brayboy (2008) describe culturally responsive approaches to schooling that draw upon the lived experiences of students, parents, and communities through the processes of schooling that center the community's core values. Further, they emphasize incorporating Indigenous languages as well as local community knowledge to make education culturally and socially engaging, relevant, and purposeful. Beyond this, the classroom contexts are also sites for learning experiences that emphasize building upon "community cultural wealth" that includes six forms of capital as the "array of knowledge, skills, abilities, and contacts possessed and utilized by communities of color to survive and resist macro and microforms of oppression" (Yosso, 2005, p. 77). In drawing upon community cultural wealth, educators of Indigenous youth help students to become critical thinkers who are engaged in their own learning. Indigenous scholar Marie Battiste (2002) writes, "[T]he distinctive features of Indigenous knowledge and pedagogy are learning by observation and doing, learning through authentic experiences and individualized instruction, and learning through enjoyment. Indigenous pedagogy accepts students' cognitive search for learning processes they can internalize" (p. 19).

The fourth feature of AIE is the integration of Western constructs of knowledge into Indigenous knowledge systems as a long-term goal of Indigenous education (Barnhardt & Kawagley, 2005; Cajete, 2012; Kawagley, 1995; Lambe, 2003; Martinez, 2010). Yet in mainstream education, there are still debates about the value of Indigenous knowledge to the contemporary experiences of Indigenous youth (Bishop, 2003; Deloria & Wildcat, 2001). For example, dominant perspectives about science stemming from positivist traditions usually derived from Euro-Western epistemologies do not recognize Indigenous ways of knowing (Lambe, 2003). Furthermore, Barnhardt and Kawagley (2005) explain the dilemma faced by Alaska Native elders as they try to identify ways to effectively utilize traditional ecological knowledge that is embedded in Native ways of knowing as a means of enriching the school curriculum and enlivening learning experiences of students.

A fifth feature of Indigenous education underscores the significance of student and teacher interactions within the process of schooling as learning and teaching practices (Klug & Whitfield, 2003; Miller Cleary & Peacock, 1998). Miller Cleary and Peacock (1998) emphasize that if teachers of Indigenous youth think of themselves as "learners, they will learn ways of being and teaching that will benefit their students" (p. 5). Additionally, Jeff Lambe (2003) states that learning from an Indigenous perspective is about a nurtured experience entirely dependent on relationships such that the notion of learning and teaching are understood as a co-process that occurs from life experiences. Further, Klug and Whitfield (2003) address this idea of becoming more interactive with students on a personal level as part of a "recursive process" of learning and teaching about and from your students (p. 23). Finally, the idea of teachers bonding with students to gain acceptance by "legitimizing personal experiences" is significant to culturally responsive approaches to teaching (Gay, 2000, p. 233). Thus, these research studies as aforementioned emphasize why positive student and teacher interactions are essential to teaching and learning for positive outcomes.

In sum, these studies on Indigenous education corroborate how these features of AIE are critical to student academic performance, positive learning outcomes, and well-being. Also, when there is an emphasis on Indigenous decolonization, liberation, and transformation, there is the potential for nurturing critical consciousness in the minds of Indigenous youth in contemporary contexts (Ah Nee-Benham, 2017; Battiste, 2013; Biermann & Townsend-Cross, 2008). Recent studies addressing contemporary issues posit an integrated, holistic, and decolonizing approach to teaching and learning (Garcia & Shirley, 2012; Smith, Tuck & Yang, 2018). That is, Indigenous educators emphasize making content knowledge relevant to students' overall experiences by thinking about the act of teaching and learning as a responsible conscious practice for decolonization and empowerment (Locke & Lindley, 2007; Trinidad, 2010).

Methodology

This critical qualitative study utilized a multiple case study design (Creswell, 1998; Strauss & Corbin, 1998) to understand how educators of Indigenous youth construct valuable insights about what constitutes CSRP. We used Tribal Critical Race Theory (TribalCrit) (Brayboy, 2005) to acknowledge the diversity of Indigenous perspectives within localized tribal community contexts. As Indigenous scholars and researchers, we positioned ourselves to emphasize how "concepts of culture, knowledge, and power take on new meaning when examined through an Indigenous lens" and the way "tribal philosophies, beliefs, customs, traditions, and visions for the future are central to understanding the lived realities of Indigenous people" (Brayboy 2005, pp. 429–430). Based on these tenets, we conjecture that the study offers critical insights about what constitutes CSRP (i.e., culturally responsive/revitalizing pedagogy as teaching and learning practices) that are informed by diverse traditional and contemporary, dynamic, and reflexive Indigenous knowledge and cultural practices.

Therefore, we started with the premise that educators of Indigenous youth who learn the history of AIE, who recognize the knowledge of their respective local communities, and who develop critical understandings about issues impacting Indigenous youth have a greater potential for becoming critically conscious educators. Based on this premise, the study examines what Indigenous pedagogy means within different tribal community contexts that are based on individual educators' constructions of knowledge and lived cultural experiences. In particular, the focus of the study is on how nine educators reflect upon their teaching practices as informed by their teacher education coursework and their own lived cultural experiences. We posit that as educators of Indigenous youth acquire new knowledge about teaching Indigenous youth, they gain important new insights when they are provided opportunities to critically reflect upon their practices.

Finally, the study highlights key considerations for articulating and/or reclaiming Indigenous-centered pedagogies within the context of education for the benefit of Indigenous youth. The primary research question is this: In what ways do educators of Indigenous youth construct new understandings of Indigenous-centered pedagogy based on their prior cultural knowledge that includes their community cultural knowledge along with newly acquired or learned academic knowledge about effective teaching and learning practices with Indigenous youth?

Data Collection and Analysis

In the study, we purposively recruited educators of Indigenous youth from diverse cultural backgrounds and a variety of educational settings who were graduate students at a research university in the U.S. Southwest. The graduate program serves primarily Indigenous graduate students who are teachers from across the nation. Overall, the program contributes to the development of professional educators working in and/or with Indigenous communities to meet the educational needs of Indigenous youth across the state and nation. In courses that are offered, students have opportunities to advance their knowledge on AIE in topics related to Indigenous education, tribal sovereignty, and language revitalization. All students in the program are encouraged to develop critical dispositions toward educating Indigenous youth by affirming the contributions of American Indian (Indigenous) cultural traditions and knowledge to the cultures of the U.S. Southwest and the world.

Using surveys and interviews, we collected data from current and former graduate students at the university where this study was conducted. First, an anonymous survey questionnaire was emailed to former and current students who took courses in the program over a 5-year period to gain insights from a larger population of students. Eighteen students out of 56 returned the survey questionnaires, providing a 45% response rate. The survey questionnaire had closed-ended items pertaining to demographic information, such as where participants were teaching currently and what content they were teaching. It also contained open-ended questions inquiring about the academic knowledge they gained from their courses in the graduate program. Survey participants were instructed at the end of the survey to contact the researchers if they were interested in participating in the post-survey interview.

The analysis of the survey questionnaires consisted of open coding and a thematic analysis of the 18 participants' responses to identify recurring themes based on what they considered to be effective practices for teaching Indigenous youth (Mason, 2002). Three overarching themes—the importance of Indigenous languages and cultures, understanding sociocultural, historical contexts, and building relationships—emerged that corroborated the review of the literature. For the second part of data collection, nine research participants were self-selected to participate in semi-structured interviews. Follow-up questions were developed from the preliminary data. The purpose of interviewing participants was to gather in-depth information about their reflections and thoughts about effectively teaching Indigenous youth. The interviews lasted 1 to 2 hours and provided an opportunity for educators to reflect upon their learning from the course content, their own teaching experiences, and how they applied that knowledge into their teaching/learning in the present contexts using their cultural knowledge.

Using axial coding (Strauss & Corbin, 1998), the researchers identified six overarching categories, each with subcategories that represented all the nine participants' responses from the interview responses about knowledge reaffirmed or new knowledge gained from the courses. For interrater reliability, both researchers coded the transcribed data separately using deductive and inductive coding and then came to an agreement about the emergent themes based on their familiarity with the empirical research and teaching AIE courses (Mason, 2002). After all data were collected and transcribed, we conducted a final analysis using selective coding to identify key relationships among all the key variables that emerged across the data sets as recurring themes (Mason, 2002). In the final analysis, we identified three findings highlighting key characteristics of Indigenous pedagogy that underscore what teachers think are culturally responsive teaching and culturally sustaining/revitalizing pedagogy when educating Indigenous youth.

Research Participants

Eight of the interview participants self-identify as Native American, while one identifies as Latina. At the time of this study, eight of the nine participants were teaching or working in some capacity with Indigenous youth. In the following section, we share their insights about effective teaching practices with the use of a pseudonym. We use pseudonyms throughout the discussion of findings.

Karen Pacheco At the time of the study, Karen was an elementary teacher from the community of San Felipe Pueblo who was finishing her graduate program. According to Karen, the courses she took that related specifically to the history of AIE "really opened [her] eyes to all the history and realities" of language loss in Native American communities. As a result of her coursework, she became very outspoken and vocal during teacher in-service trainings about the importance of embracing all students as your own children and moving away from a deficit view of students.

Melanie Arquero Melanie identifies as Acoma, Zia, and Zuni Pueblo, representing three different Indigenous nations. She emphasized that they are all very important to her self-identity. Throughout the interviews, she stressed the connection between language, culture, and identity. Although she was not teaching at the time of the study, she shared much about her past teaching practices and philosophy, which was largely informed by her own understanding of Indigenous knowledge. As an Indigenous activist, she was prompted to advocate for her students' rights to their language and culture-based education.

Reina Calabaza Reina is a young Diné (Navajo)[2] teacher who taught in the local urban school district. She was a new high school math teacher at the time of the study. Many of her responses in the interviews revealed that she was drawing a lot from her own experiences as a student as well as the new knowledge she gained from courses that helped construct new understandings about teaching for herself. Reina stated, "I know that every kid, they are able to learn. They have the skills to learn but they all learn differently. I knew that one thing that I had to do with them was understand where they come from [and get] to know what community they are from and what they do on a daily basis with their family." In doing so, Reina highlights the significance of getting to know her students, which is at the heart of her new understanding.

Yanni Vanderwagon Yanni is a Diné (Navajo) woman with a background in art and English literature that allowed her to work as a visiting artist for an afterschool program. Her commitment to working with Indigenous youth was inspired by her own work as a renowned artist and poet. Yanni received a master's degree in art education but took several AIE courses because of her interest in the topic. At the time of the study, she was working as a substitute teacher for an art program that was part of a writing project emphasizing literacy and the arts. She shared how art education can be a powerful motivator for her in working with students, especially in how it provides insights to students to reassert a cultural identity and for pursuing knowledge that will help them in the future.

Carla Alvarez Carla self-identifies as Latina. She volunteered to participate in this study because of her strong interest in working with Indigenous youth. At the time of the study, she was teaching undergraduate courses to Indigenous youth at a branch campus. She talked about some of her own effective practices of working with Indigenous youth at the university level. Carla stated, "I would always model my own culture, my own examination of my own culture and growing up in it."

Janet Shorty At the time of the study, Janet was one of the few Diné (Navajo) language teachers in the school district where she worked. She shared some of her challenges and frustrations with teaching an Indigenous language in a large metropolitan city. However, she also discussed what she saw from working with the parents of students that highlighted a different sense of parent engagement. That is, she talked about helping students and their parents instill a positive sense of cultural identity by sharing what she learned from her own education and helping them to understand that their feelings about education do not have to be negative.

Bradley Nelson Bradley is one of several participants who is not native to the state where this study was conducted. However, he has lived in the area for a long time and is very much committed to serving Indigenous youth at the local university branch campus, where he works primarily as a counselor and adjunct faculty. As a member of the Hopi and Shawnee nations, he served in the military before completing a Bachelor of Arts degree in education. He explained that through his military training, he was able to learn about the world and acquire skills that he felt were needed by Indigenous youth to be successful in a global world.

Whitney Morgan Whitney was also a Diné language teacher at the time of the study teaching in a charter school for Indigenous youth. Whitney's passion for teaching evolved over time because she wanted to relearn and learn more about her language and ways to teach the language. Whitney stated,

> I felt like I didn't have a place to use my language and I found myself moving away from that until I started taking [courses] to help me understand just my inner and external being and started finally accepting that . . . when I started learning about Indigenous education . . . it made it more exciting when I learned from the Indigenous perspective.

Whitney's comment that Indigenous education focuses on what she knows from home underscores the way educators of Indigenous youth can often draw upon their own perspectives.

Grace Robideaux Grace is Diné and a member of a northern tribe who was the only participant who did not live in the state at the time of the study, so all her responses to the interview questions were completed via written email responses. During the study, she was volunteering as a language teacher for her tribe. She served as the director of her tribe's language program and attributes much of her success to her learning new knowledge from the AIE courses. Grace stated,

> My understanding has changed drastically. I see the oppression that has a grasp on Native people. This change to help our Native people has to come from within communities and from this, the most intimate work has to be done by community members/insiders. I have utilized a good portion of what I learned in my classes to help my tribe.

In sum, the nine participants' responses confirm past research about effective practices that highlight student and teacher relationships; culturally responsive schooling; an acknowledgment of the legacies and remnants of oppression; and the integration of Indigenous and Western knowledge (Gay, 2000; Kawagley, 1995; Klug & Whitfield, 2003; Miller Cleary & Peacock, 1998). However, the main intent of this study was to go beyond identifying exemplary practices for teaching Indigenous youth by examining the different ways that teachers of Indigenous youth construct new insights and/or meanings about what constitutes Indigenous pedagogy in contemporary contexts.

Findings

Three findings emerged from the overall study that highlight the significance of educators' insights into Indigenous pedagogy based upon their own reflections about teaching as well as drawing upon their lived cultural experiences. They are (1) content knowledge integration, (2) student and teacher relationships, and (3) educators' reflective thinking.

Content Knowledge Integration

One key finding underscores how these nine educators of Indigenous youth affirmed the importance of Indigenous knowledge to the learning experiences of Indigenous youth as well as their own teaching practices. For example, in the following statements Grace, Melanie, and Yanni discussed the ways that Indigenous youth benefit from having their knowledge (i.e., cultural experiences, history, and language) included in school curriculum.

> **Grace:** When Native ways of knowing are incorporated while educating our Native youth, there is an immediate change in wellbeing and a stronger sense of understanding with a grounded identity. Culturally relevant materials will help Native children connect more academically and to fuse the gap between home life and school life.
>
> **Melanie:** Native students often come in already knowing the core values of their tribe because they've been taught . . . it is their way of being. Their way of being is to be appreciated.
>
> **Yanni:** I feel the best way to approach this issue is to present the subject with both points of view/experience via American historical facts. This concept is really about enacting the way knowledge becomes power for the individual to succeed.

Just as previous research called for the maintenance of Native (Indigenous) languages and culture in school curricula (Klug & Whitfield, 2003; McCarty, Romero-Little, & Zepeda, 2013), research participants in this study also advocated for more integration of Indigenous language and culture in the contemporary contexts because it helps to affirm a cultural identity and sense of self-worth.

Several participants discussed how they engaged in critical dialogue with their students and parents. They shared examples of how the intergenerational transmission of Indigenous languages and cultural knowledge were disrupted in many Indigenous communities due to the legacies and remnants of oppression. Furthermore, they shared how they approach culturally sensitive topics like intergenerational trauma that continues to impact the contemporary lives of Indigenous youth (Yellow Horse Brave Heart, 1998).

> **Melanie:** I had not heard of historical or intergenerational trauma until I came to the university where I enrolled in Indigenous courses taught by Indigenous instructors. When these ideas were brought to my attention, I felt they made a lot of sense. In designing curriculum and planning lessons, my first intention is to have the lesson demonstrate how local tribal people contributed to the knowledge so that Native students recognized, acknowledged, and felt pride. I would do that before I presented the American version; then, I would ask questions that helped students think critically and compare the differences. In doing this, Native students take ownership of their tribal contributions. Doing this begins the healing and the building of self-confidence.
>
> **Whitney:** When we talk about articles that I read about . . . Intergenerational trauma, Intergenerational healing . . . I also notice that some of our students, it's hard for their guardians to speak out and say, "Ok, maybe if I talk about it, I will start healing." When I teach language and culture, I try to send that back with my students so that they can teach their parents . . . they come back and some of them will say, "You know in my community, this is how I was taught or this is what I was taught," or "Oh, I never knew that." Or parents would email me and say, "I never knew this! Thank you for sharing this with my daughter, my son!!"

Finally, Melanie and Whitney explained how a critical understanding of past historical, sociocultural, and political issues help them as teachers to talk about these topics related to historical trauma with students and parents as a way to heal from the past in relation to their contemporary experiences (Yellow Horse Brave Heart, 1998). For example, Janet shared her perspective on becoming more reflective as well as critical in her thinking and sharing those traits with her students:

> **Janet:** I am not sure if reflexive thinking is unique to Indigenous thought. But I think it is potentially a by-product of growing up within a culture that tried to marginalize you. What I learned is that you can learn about concepts without privileging one culture's understanding of that concept over another. So, I do think that my pedagogy comes from how I learned to assimilate knowledge and how to see the world as full of many perspectives.

In different ways, each of these educators described how they use a culturally responsive approach and culturally sustaining/revitalizing pedagogy to engage students and parents in critical dialogue pertaining to significant issues impacting the communities. Moreover, the participants shared how they reflect upon their own dispositions (as teachers, parents, and even community members) when teaching and learning from these interactions. In doing so, they are able to integrate important knowledge that is powerful for the students and parents to recognize, like the impact of historical trauma on Indigenous communities and how education was used in the past for assimilation. This reveals how these educators draw upon their lived cultural experiences to inform their teaching methods. Overall, these practices resonate with tenets of TribalCrit by acknowledging the legacies of colonization and privileging and using Indigenous knowledge to address contemporary issues.

Student and Teacher Relationships

Another finding from this study highlights the way in which teachers consider student and teacher relationships and/or interactions that extend beyond the classroom and into the community. Karen shared a story of what she said to non-Native teachers who were new to her community, who often had a difficult time with students because of their lack of respect and/or understanding regarding the cultural background of their students.

> **Karen:** I said, "Can you not see how you are treating our children? Can you not even realize maybe they are having these behaviors because that's what you are giving to them? If you are not giving them respect, they are not going to respect you. That is . . . like a whole another thing. If you are not teaching them to be a community, you are not teaching them."

Reina also expressed how she believed that teachers who work with Indigenous youth must embrace the larger community's values of respect in order to receive respect from students.

> **Reina:** I think a lot of them are looking for that big word, Respect. You know . . . that's taught in our culture that we have to respect our elders. And a lot of Native American students can't . . . either they are not respecting their teacher, or they just can't respect them because they

are not respecting them back. I think that is why a lot of them are quiet. That's why a lot of them are scared to ask for help or go to office hours for the teacher.

In these responses, Karen and Reina expressed why they believe that some students have trouble "respecting" their teachers because they do not feel like they are respected in return.

Several participants also elaborated on the concept of mutual respect that must be developed between teachers and students to allow for any transformation to occur. For example, Janet and Whitney both described the influence of k'é (the Diné concept of acknowledging and honoring community relationships) to their own practices and process for teaching. In drawn-out responses, both teachers discussed at length what k'é means to them and how it is a key to their success of engaging students. For example, Janet commented that "it is meaningful to the students as young as kindergarten to have a program like mine because they get to be with their own." Thereby, in being with others who are like them, students show more enthusiasm and motivation to learn.

Some participants also expressed how community and/or parent engagement must be reconsidered in the process of getting to know students, which can eventually help to develop and establish more trust and respect among all of them. For example, Karen emphasized community and parent engagement by sharing how she developed her lessons based on her students' interests and lived experiences using an integrated approach or, as she described it, in a holistic way of teaching "so it's not in bits and pieces." She elaborated on her practice of focusing on themes like family to teach math, science, and language arts through a culturally responsive approach.

Last, Melanie provided additional insights about what it means to be respectful based on her cultural understanding/experiences and how these notions of respect inform her interactions with her students.

> There is always the element of respect, cooperation, helping others, and acknowledgment. I don't know what other tribes do to initiate their youth into adulthood. In Pueblo communities, spiritual and tribal leaders at every community function remind us to be respectful, truthful, honest, and being decent human beings. Their advice is what I followed when I was teaching and still follow in my own life. These teachings are what I continue to impart in the classroom often. I take time to explain that respect, cooperation, and helping others go together . . . So, the message . . . I remind them, is to be the helpful brother, sister, cousin,

or friend. As teachers who were taught our way of life by our families or within the community, we need to draw on how we were taught.

Similarly, Karen shared her insights about respecting her students by drawing upon their local cultural knowledge with regard to discipline. She described how she collaborates with her students to define the classroom rules, which in turn allows the youth to reflect upon/think about their actions, make new choices, and take responsibility for their learning. This approach reminds us that "the primary tenet of TribalCrit is the notion that colonization is endemic to society" (Brayboy, 2005, p. 430), such that any notions of respect and/or civility in schools are often framed from a Eurocentric paradigm. In Melanie and Karen's analyses of their own and their students' lived experiences, they are challenging mainstream notions of respect by explaining it from their own epistemological and ontological views largely based on the local community's cultural core values.

Reflective Thinking

The third finding from this study highlights the practice of critical reflective thinking (Ladson-Billings, 1994). Some of the participants described how they reflect on their own sense of self-identity and well-being and/or positionality (i.e., disposition). Yanni shared her thoughts:

Indigenous pedagogy demands that the educator/teacher use every means to integrate cultural beliefs and customs into their curriculum and classroom. Teachers/educators need to live by example in what they believe to be true. Simple ways of tangibly doing this may be by including imagery of Indigenous leaders and community people in their classroom décor or using cultural music as a part of their daily classroom ritual. Personally, it may be by showing cultural heritage in dress and personal adornment practices via jewelry and hairstyle. As educator's we are the example our Indigenous children see on a daily basis, what we do, say, act, model are reflected onto the students.

Yanni underscored the notion of being or becoming culturally grounded. Her comment about living by example for young people reveals that cultural humility and pride are essential to an educator's commitment and responsibility to their students as well as themselves based within an understanding of teaching and learning for life's sake. Moreover, this statement reinforces the need for teachers to continue their own lifelong search for cultural knowledge and languages just as they are encouraging their students to learn/grow over their lifetime.

As these educators of Indigenous youth reconnect with Indigenous-centered perspectives about teaching and learning, they, in turn, help Indigenous youth achieve a critical sense of who they are, where their place is in the community and the world, and what they are learning with respect to their lives. For example, Yanni described using Indigenous art, stories, and music, embedded with Indigenous epistemologies, to draw on her lived cultural experiences as an artist to relate to her students' interests and motivations for learning about themselves and their community. This process of continued learning can be attributed to the process of reflective thinking that is crucial for teachers and educators who advocate for culturally sustaining/revitalizing pedagogies. In this way, she was able to understand what it means to be a teacher vis-à-vis a learner who is striving to make transformational changes and have a positive influence on the lives of the youth.

On reflective thinking, Karen shared her thoughts about using prayers in schools to connect to and support students' overall learning experiences in the schools as well to the larger community and the natural world.

> **Karen:** When I got my license to teach the Native American language, they asked me: "What do you feel about teaching prayer in classrooms?" And I told them, it is a double-edged sword because we are damned if we do and we are damned if we don't. I tell them I would teach how you begin, how you would what you say to begin and that is as far as I would go . . . because prayers come from the heart. I can't teach or tell this child what to believe . . . Otherwise, I would probably just . . . I teach protocols. But we can talk about protocols or how to behave and all that until we are blue in the face . . . but until you take that child and actually sit with them during a dance and actually show them this is how we behave, and they are actually doing it and see why then they are going to learn. Instead of talking, lecturing, and stuff like that . . . I could talk all day and they are just going to sit there . . . so when we sit at an assembly, I tell them to remember this is just like when you are praying. You are quiet, keep your hands to yourself . . . close your eyes and pray, listen to what they are talking about.

In the statements from Karen and Yanni about motivating young people to learn about their cultural identity and the local community's expected sociocultural norms, they highlight the idea of role modeling by demonstrating expected behaviors and core values of being respectful, humble, and reverent. This approach was also discussed by Melanie with respect to teaching Indigenous youth to draw upon their sense of self and well-being that makes them feel connected to their learning.

Melanie: Intuition is beyond the usual senses we're often reminded of, especially in science classes. Intuition seems to be developed early on. I think we are still connected with Creation at the time of birth and intuition continues in an environment where Indigenous people already have it, have a sense of things, and have a knowing. It's important to look at intuition that is present in our Native students . . . it shows up as a gut reaction to something. When they are given a task, especially out in nature, they are so quick to act on their intuition and are often correct . . . I just use my intuition and connect with theirs. We look at the whole. We think. We visualize. Questions come. We ask. We guess. We analyze. We discuss. We reference storytelling. We compare one thing to another. Our thinking connects with our spirit teachers, guides, and helpers. We continue to think about it. We go into daydreaming. It's okay for students to daydream. They are connecting with their spirit teachers, guides, and helpers in that state and may be receiving information.

Finally, the notion of lighting an internal flame for learning is prominent in the idea of educating "the inner self through enlivenment and illumination from one's own being and the learning of key relationships" (Cajete, 1994, p. 34). Thus, even if students are not strongly informed about their cultural traditions or do not speak their Native languages, educators can still guide and mentor them to embrace innate cultural characteristics essential for learning that were already planted within them through their ancestors' blood and teachings (i.e., genetic memory). Thus, educators must tap into the lived experiences of Indigenous youth coming from different cultural backgrounds who bring with them different perspectives based on their own cultural lifeways, values, and beliefs. In sum, the participants' responses reveal that Indigenous knowledge is "community cultural wealth" (Yosso, 2005), which teachers and students must acknowledge, recognize, and utilize in teaching and learning. Moreover, within the idea of CSPR is the practice of educators themselves coming to a realization about who they are, where they come from, and why they are teaching. In turn, the courses provided at this institution unconsciously and consciously provide new teachings that are culturally relevant and bring issues to the forefront that are sometimes swept under the rug and often left out (e.g., historical trauma). This act of consciousness-raising allows educators to strive to learn more about their own cultural knowledge and to deeply reflect upon their own teaching practices.

Discussion

In this section we discuss further how educators of Indigenous youth construct renewed understandings about what constitutes Indigenous pedagogies by reflecting on their teaching and learning through a process of synthesizing new experiences with traditional knowledge. In addition to incorporating Indigenous traditional cultural knowledge into students' learning experiences to make the learning relevant, all the participants described different ways they helped students to reaffirm their own sense of self-identity and well-being by reflecting on their own lived experiences. This was evident in responses from Yanni, Karen, and Melanie in describing the importance of teachers to become culturally responsive and/or grounded in their own local community Indigenous knowledge. Thus, developing cultural humility and cultural pride is essential to any educator who wants to make a commitment to the students and the communities. Furthermore, as expressed by several participants, cultural groundedness can be modeled by teachers through their teaching practices, their critical agency to speak out for others, their overall sense of maintaining a cultural identity, and everyday interactions and behaviors with students. However, this requires taking on the responsibility to learn more about themselves as part of the critical reflections that are needed about their role within the relationship between teaching and learning.

The participants also described in different ways how Indigenous pedagogy aligns with social constructivist paradigms (Brooks & Brooks, 1993; Vygotsky, 1980). Indigenous pedagogy emphasizes social and cultural contexts for learning and teaching for cognitive and social development. One participant, Yanni, for example, articulated how helping her students affirm a sense of identity and purpose in their lives is like lighting "a little candle in their hearts." This statement underscores traditional Diné teachings of inspiration and/or personal motivation by stating, *t'áá hó'ajitéego* ("it is up to you"). This statement is about self-empowerment and self-identity for achieving balance and harmony. For example, Dr. Wilson Aronilth (1999) describes Diné centered pedagogy as essential to Diné youths' attitudes, capabilities, and motivations for learning and a sense of trust/respect for self within specific cultural and social processes of learning and teaching.

Overall, these findings underscore TribalCrit as providing a critical reflective lens that posits a recentering of Indigenous knowledge within school curriculum and reconceptualizing Indigenous education through an Indigenous lens that entails a critical process of reflective thinking and ongoing synthesis of knowledge. In particular, these nine educators' insights, based on their narratives about CSRP, highlight the significance of drawing upon their cultural background knowledge, lived experiences, and localized Indigenous core values to inform their teaching and learning practices. More so, by acknowledging legacies of oppression, educators of Indigenous youth provide a space for critical dialogue and opportunities for their students to act, think, and reflect critically about their identity, their community's history, and different ways to address the challenges presented (Bodkin-Andrews & Carlson, 2016; Klug & Whitfield, 2003).

This study posits that educators of Indigenous youth who strive to reconnect with, reclaim, and/or recover Indigenous-centered perspectives about teaching and learning help Indigenous youth achieve a critical sense of self, place, and educational subject matter with respect to their lives or "education for life's sake" (Cajete, 1994, p. 6). From a Navajo paradigm, teaching and learning are not opposites but complementary. That is, teaching and learning are interrelated and coexist on a cyclical "merging continuum" of experiences and meaning-making that reflect natural, creative processes (Maryboy, Begay, & Nichol, 2020). Thus, teaching and learning are a continuum of how a learner and teacher interact and/or relate with one another that informs and becomes foundational to a "dynamic equilibrium," where there is "not hierarchy or polarity . . . similar to the unified cosmic process inherent in the natural cycles of night and day . . . becoming visible and clear to the human consciousness" (p. 18). This is different from Western paradigms that often perceive teaching and learning from a linear perspective, resulting in a dichotomy or oppositional forces.

The participants revealed that their unique understandings of what constitutes Indigenous pedagogy are best informed by specific cultural understandings about what teaching and learning mean within each and every Indigenous community and cultural context (Battiste, 2013; Brayboy, 2005; Yosso, 2005). Additionally, the findings underscore the ways in which educators of Indigenous youth construct Indigenous pedagogy as culturally sustaining/revitalizing pedagogy (McCarty & Lee, 2014). Thus, the significance of educators building up, drawing upon, and integrating their own cultural knowledge and lived experiences with newly acquired knowledge is central to Indigenous youths' success in schools.

In the long run, when Indigenous youth see the importance of learning/ teaching that is significant to who they are, who they want to be, as well as who they should be based on their own, their families, and community's conception of being "educated" (Martinez, 2010); they begin to accept that education can be liberating and/or transformative (Freire, 2000). At the heart of this are the relationships and interactions between learners and educators as a way of reaffirming who they are, where their place is in the community as well as the world, and why they seek or share knowledge for life's sake. Brayboy (2005) reminds us that

> knowledge is defined by TribalCrit as the ability to recognize change, adapt, and move forward with the change. For many Indigenous people, culture is rooted to lands on which they live as well as to their ancestors who lived on those lands before them. (p. 434)

Indigenous peoples are resilient and return to ancestral teachings as it provides stability and a foundation to life.

Finally, the study highlights how positive teacher dispositions entail affirming a critical culturally sustaining/revitalizing approach to teaching and learning that involves getting to know communities, parents, students, and, more importantly, teachers' own culturally mediated learning experiences that are informed by their Indigenous cultural and linguistic backgrounds. The key features of Indigenous pedagogy can provide a reflective lens for teachers of Indigenous youth to look critically and reflexively at their teaching practices (methodologies, strategies, and approaches) and transform these practices to meet their students' needs and potential while also embracing their own new understandings that are informed from both Indigenous and Western perspectives about teaching and learning. There is a need for more research about teaching and learning from Indigenous perspectives that integrate Indigenous language and culture into students' learning experiences. This requires a theoretical lens like TribalCrit as well as a unique process of critical reflection for rearticulating the goals of Indigenous education that include a re-envisioning and an Indigenous transformative politics to meet the challenges of yesterday and tomorrow.

Conclusion

The three findings that emerged from the study highlight (1) the integration of Indigenous language and cultural knowledge with Euro-Western content knowledge in school curriculum, (2) the reaffirmation of student and teacher relationships as a dialectical process of pedagogy, and (3) the process of reflective synthesis by educators that is necessary for practicing culturally sustaining pedagogy.

We shared key insights from this study using Tribal Critical Race Theory about what constitutes Indigenous pedagogies based on the different ways educators of Indigenous youth construct their learning and teaching practices through processes of critical reflection of newly acquired academic knowledge and their cultural background and experiences with the goal of transformation and critical consciousness-raising (Biermann & Townsend-Cross, 2008; McCarty & Lee, 2014; Werito, 2016). Based on interviews with nine educators of Indigenous youth who shared their perspectives through reflective insights about what it means to teach Indigenous youth, this study offers a depth of knowledge that contributes to existing research in understanding the different ways that teachers construct engaging and culturally relevant learning practices for Indigenous youth from their own perspectives.

Indigenous culture- and place-based educational models informed by critical Indigenous perspectives like environmental Indigenous pedagogy and critical educational studies are needed for teaching Indigenous youth (Apple, 2000; Biermann & Townsend-Cross, 2008; Grande, 2004). It is important to acknowledge that place-based educational models that call for a return to "land-based practices" are crucial to Indigenous decolonization and liberation agendas (Alfred, 2009) and may look different across Indigenous communities within urban or rural tribal sociocultural contexts that warrants further research.

The study maintains that when key features of Indigenous pedagogy are acknowledged, practiced, and used to help Indigenous youth learn about who they are while moving them from cultural awareness to individual awareness for community empowerment, the youth become more culturally grounded, critically conscious, and more informed of their cultural perspectives, education, and life opportunities.

Vincent Werito (Diné) is associate professor in the Department of Language, Literacy and Sociocultural Studies at the University of New Mexico. His research interests are in Diné education, critical race theory, bilingual education, Indigenous language revitalization, Indigenous research methodologies, culturally responsive pedagogies, social justice education, and transformative Indigenous educational models.

Vangee Nez (Diné) earned her PhD from the Department of Language, Literacy and Sociocultural Studies at the University of New Mexico. She is an

Indigenous Language & Educational Consultant and was the former Site Coordinator for the Navajo Technical University at the Kirtland Instructional Site in Kirtland, New Mexico.

NOTES

1 Throughout the article, we use the term *Indigenous* as synonymous with *American Indian, Native,* or *Native American,* with reference to the original peoples of North America.

2 We use the term *Diné* as synonymous with *Navajo. Diné* means "The People" in the Navajo language and refers to the way Navajo people describe themselves in their own language.

REFERENCES

Ah Nee-Benham, M. K. P. (2017). *Indigenous educational models for contemporary practice: In our mother's voice* (Vol. II). Routledge.

Alfred, G. T. (2009). Colonialism and state dependency. *Journal of Aboriginal Health, 5*(2), 42–60.

Apple, M. W. (2000). *Official knowledge: Democratic education in a conservatist age* (2nd ed.). Routledge.

Aronilth, W., Jr. (1999). *An introduction to Navajo philosophy* (4th ed.). Diné College.

Barnhardt, R., & Kawagley, A. O. (2005). Indigenous knowledge systems and Alaska Native ways of knowing. *Anthropology and Education Quarterly, 36*(1), 8–23.

Battiste, M. (2002). *Indigenous knowledge and pedagogy in First Nations education: Literature review with recommendations.* National Working Group on Education and the Minister of Indian Affairs, Indian and Northern Affairs (INAC).

Battiste, M. (2013). *Decolonizing education: Nourishing the learning spirit.* Purich.

Bergstrom, A., Miller Cleary, L., & Peacock T. (2003). *The seventh generation: Native students speak about finding the good path.* ERIC Clearinghouse on Rural Education and Small Schools.

Biermann, S., & Townsend-Cross, M. (2008). Indigenous pedagogy as a force of change. *The Australian Journal of Indigenous Education, 37,* 146–154.

Bishop, R. (2003). Changing power relations in education: Kuapapa Maori messages for "mainstream" education in Aotearoa/New Zealand. *Comparative Education, 39*(2), 221–238. https://doi.org/10.1080/03050060302555

Bodkin-Andrews, G., & Carlson, B. (2016). The legacy of racism and Indigenous Australian identity within education. *Race, Ethnicity, and Education, 19*(4), 784–807.

Brayboy, B. M. J. (2005). Toward a Tribal Critical Race Theory in education. *The Urban Review, 37*(5), 425–446.

Brooks, J. G., & Brooks, M. G. (1993). *In search of understanding: The case for constructivist classrooms.* Association for Supervision and Curriculum Development.

Cajete, G. (1994). *Look to the mountain: An ecology of Indigenous education*. Kivaki Press.

Cajete, G. (1999). *Igniting the sparkle: An Indigenous science education model*. Kivaki Press.

Cajete, G. (2012). *Decolonizing Indigenous education in the twenty-first century. For Indigenous minds only*. School for Advanced Research.

Castagno, A. E., & Brayboy, B. M. J. (2008). Culturally responsive schooling for Indigenous youth: A review of the literature. *Review of Educational Research, 78*(4), 941–993.

Castagno, A. E., & Brayboy, B. M. J. (2009). Self-determination through self-education: Culturally responsive schooling for Indigenous students in the USA. *Teacher Education, 20*(1), 31–53.

Creswell, J. (1998). *Qualitative inquiry and research design: Choosing among five traditions*. SAGE.

Deloria, V. Jr. & Wildcat, D. (2001). *Power and place: Indian education in America*. Fulcrum.

Demmert, W. G., Jr. (2001). *Improving academic performance among Native American students: a review of the research literature*. ERIC Clearinghouse on Rural Education and Small Schools.

Freire, P. (2000). *Pedagogy of the oppressed* (2nd ed.). Continuum.

Garcia, J., & Shirley, V. (2012). Performing decolonization: Lessons learned from Indigenous youth, teachers, and leader' engagement with critical Indigenous pedagogy. *Journal of Curriculum Theorizing, 28*(2), 76–91.

Gay, G. (2000). *Culturally responsive teaching: Theory, research, and practice*. Teachers College Press.

Grande, S. (2004). *Red pedagogy: Native American social and political thought*. Rowman and Littlefield.

Harrison, N., & Greenfield, M. (2011). Relationship to place: Positioning Aboriginal knowledge and perspectives in classroom pedagogies. *Critical Studies in Education, 52*(1), 65–76.

Haynes Writer, J. (2012). The savage within: No child left behind—again and again. In B. Klug (Ed.), *Standing together: American Indian education* (pp. 55–70). Rowman and Littlefield.

Kawagley, A. O. (1995). *A Yupiak worldview: A pathway to ecology and spirit*. Waveland Press.

Klug, B. J., & Whitfield, P. T. (2003). *Widening the circle: Culturally relevant pedagogy for American Indian children*. Routledge. https://doi.org/10.4324/9780203616703

Ladson-Billings, G. (1994). Who will teach our children? Preparing teachers to successfully teach African American students. In E. R. Hollins, J. E. King, & W. Hayman (Eds.), *Teaching diverse populations: Formulating a knowledge base* (pp. 129–157). SUNY Press.

Ladson-Billings, G. (2009). *The dreamkeepers: Successful teachers of African American children*. Jossey-Bass.

Lambe, J. (2003). Indigenous education, mainstream education, and Native studies: Some considerations when incorporating Indigenous pedagogy into Native studies. *American Indian Quarterly, 27*(1/2), 308–324.

Lipka, J., Mohatt, G., & The Ciulistet Group. (1998). *Transforming the culture of schools: Yupik Eskimo examples*. Lawrence Erlbaum.

Locke, S., & Lindley, L. (2007). Rethinking social studies for a critical democracy in American Indian/Alaska Native education. *Journal of American Indian Education, 46*(1), 1–19.

Lomawaima, K. T., & McCarty, T. L. (2006). *"To remain an Indian": Lessons in democracy from a century of Native American education*. Teachers College Press.

Martinez, G. (2010). *Native pride: The politics of curriculum and instruction in an urban public school*. Hampton Press.

Maryboy, N., Begay, D., & Nichol, L. (2020). Paradox and transformation. *International Journal of Applied Science and Sustainable Development, 2*(1), 15–24.

Mason, J. (2002). *Qualitative researching* (2nd ed.). SAGE.

McCarty, T. L., & Lee, T. S. (2014). Critical culturally sustaining/revitalizing pedagogy and Indigenous education sovereignty. *Harvard Educational Review, 84*(1), 101–124.

McCarty, T. L., & Lee, T. S. (2015). The role of schools in Native American language and culture revitalization. In W. Jacob, S. Cheng, & M. Porter (Eds.), *Indigenous education: Language, culture and identity* (pp. 341–360). Springer.

McCarty, T. L., Romero-Little, E., Warhol, L., & Zepeda, O. (2013). Language in the lives of Indigenous youth. In T. L. McCarty, *Language planning and policy in Native America: History, theory and praxis* (pp. 156–182). Multilingual Matters.

Miller Cleary, L., & Peacock, T. D. (1998). *Collected wisdom: American Indian education*. Allyn and Bacon.

Minthorn, R. (2016). Strengthening our teaching by honoring our culture. In A. F. Chavez & S. D. Longerbeam (Eds.), *Going inward: The role of cultural introspection in college teaching* (pp. 200–206). Peter Lang.

Ngai, P., & Koehn, P. (2011). Indigenous education for critical democracy: Teacher approaches and learning outcomes in a K-5 Indian Education for All program. *Equity and Excellence, 44*(2), 249–269.

Paris, D. (2012). Culturally sustaining pedagogy: A needed change in stance, terminology, and practice. *Educational Researcher, 41*(3), 93–97.

Paris, D. & Alim, H. S., (2017). *Culturally Sustaining Pedagogies: Teaching and Learning for Justice in a Changing World*. Teachers College Press.

Pewewardy, C. (2002). Learning styles of American Indian/Alaska Native Students: A review of the research and implications for practice. *Journal of American Indian Education, 41*(3), 22–56.

Pirbhai-Illich, F., Pete, S., & Martin, F. (2017). *Culturally responsive pedagogy: Working towards decolonization, Indigeneity, and interculturalism*. Palgrave Macmillan.

Rahman, K. (2013). Belonging and learning to belong in school: The implications of the hidden curriculum for indigenous students. *Discourse: Studies in Cultural Politics of Education, 34*(5), 660–676.

Reyhner, J., & Eder, J. (2004). *American Indian education: A history* (2nd ed.). University of Oklahoma Press.

Smith, L. T., Tuck, E., & Yang, W. K. (2018). *Indigenous and decolonizing studies in education: Mapping the long view*. Routledge.

Spring, J. (2007). *Deculturalization and the struggle for equality: A brief history of dominated cultures in the United States* (5th ed.). McGraw-Hill.

Strauss, A., & Corbin, J. (1998). *Basics of qualitative research: Techniques and procedures for developing ground theory* (2nd ed.). SAGE.

Suina, J. (2004). Native language teachers in a struggle for language and cultural survival. *Anthropology and Education Quarterly, 35*(3), 281–302.

Szasz, M. C. (1999). *Education and the American Indian: The road to self-determination, 1928-1998.* University of New Mexico Press.

Trinidad, A. M. O. (2010). Critical indigenous pedagogy: A framework to Indigenize a youth food justice movement. *Journal of Indigenous Social Development, 1*(1), 1–17.

Vygotsky, L. S. (1980). *Mind in society: The development of higher psychological processes.* Harvard University Press.

Werito, V. (2016). Education is our horse: On the path to critical consciousness in teaching and learning. In S. D. Longerbeam & A. F. Chavez (Eds.), *Going inward: The role of cultural introspection in college teaching* (pp. 67–73). Peter Lang Publishing.

Yellow Horse Brave Heart, M. (1998). The return to the sacred path: Healing the historical trauma and historical unresolved grief response among the Lakota. *Smith College Studies in Social Work, 68*(3), 287–305.

Yosso, T. J. (2005). Whose culture has capital? A critical race theory discussion of community cultural wealth. *Race, Ethnicity, and Education, 8*(1), 69–91.

"You're Not Going to Round Me to Zero, You're Going to Round Me to at Least One, I Will at Least Be One": Lumbee Erasure, Identity, and Stories of a Lumbee Professor and a Lumbee Student

BRITTANY DANIELLE HUNT AND MEGAN LOCKLEAR

This work centers on the experiences of a Lumbee lecturer and a Lumbee student at a large university in the southeastern United States. The Lumbee lecturer had never taught a Native student, and the Lumbee student had never had a Native professor. This work details their experiences in this context and explores the importance of Lumbee identity for both scholars, while also centering their struggles in the academy and their resistance and resilience to it. A major theme of this work is the importance of representation, both for students and their teachers. This work is guided by Tribal Critical Race Theory.

Introduction

In the summer of 2019, as I (Hunt) began reviewing my roster for the Social Work Diversity class I would teach that semester, I noticed something that would be a turning point for me: a Lumbee student had enrolled in one of my classes. I am a member of the Lumbee Tribe of North Carolina, which is the largest tribe east of the Mississippi River and the ninth-largest in the nation (Lumbee Tribe, 2016). Despite these numbers, Lumbees living in urban areas are often plagued with a level of obscurity that they do not experience in their tribal communities. The struggle to find other Natives in the city can be daunting and desperate. When I saw my student's last name, I knew that she was Lumbee like me. Lumbees number in the 60,000s but are bound by a rather condensed set of last names, including Locklear, Hunt, Oxendine, and Lowery, to name a few (Lowery, 2018). Her name was Megan Locklear, and I knew instinctively that she was Lumbee. So, I let out a yelp of excitement because she would be the very first Native student, and Lumbee specifically, whom I would teach.

On our first day of class, I felt a nervousness and responsibility that I had not yet felt as a professor. I enjoyed teaching immensely prior to this, but in teaching non-Native students about Native history and realities within the context of the social work course, I had previously focused mostly on helping students to unlearn the stereotypes that they held about Native people. Locklear though, likely would not have those same stereotypes. Therefore, the Native content I provided in class would have to go beyond correcting miseducation; it would need to more fully articulate her identity as Native and as Lumbee, specifically, within the context of social work. I knew Megan was probably learning very little, if anything, in her other courses about American Indian people, and I wanted to provide her with as much content as possible in my course, while still attending to the greater theme of "diversity." In my experience, when I was an undergraduate like Megan, professors often either ignored Indigenous people completely when creating course content or delivered information that was inaccurate or deeply problematic. I wanted to provide Megan a respite from the otherwise anti-Indigenous overtones of academia.

In addition to being a part-time professor, I was also a PhD student at the university. At our university, there are currently 29,615 students. Of those students, 0.27% are American Indian (n=79) (Institutional Research Analytics, 2020). In the University's *Progress Report of Campus Plan for Diversity*, there is a note stating, "[T]he first to second-year retention rates for first-time-in-college students (FTIC) exceed 81% for all groups except American Indians. Since 2013, graduation rates have increased for all groups except American Indians" (UNC Charlotte, 2019, p. 2). Though American Indians account for 1% of all staff on campus, there are no numbers provided for faculty. There is a note stating that "groups constituting less than 1% of hiring have been omitted" (p. 13); the last Native professor reported by the university taught in 2009 (Office of Institutional Research, 2009). I am currently the only Native American PhD student at the university (Institutional Research Analytics, 2020), and, to my knowledge, the only Native American professor on campus, albeit as an adjunct.

Before meeting Locklear, I had recently come to the realization that, although I have an undergraduate degree and a master's degree and am in the final stages of my doctoral degree, I will never have had a Native professor for the entirety of my studies. This realization was a sobering one for me. However, perhaps there is a greater joy underscoring the discontent. I will never get to have a Native professor, but I get to be one to a Native student. As Native women, we do not always get the flowers; sometimes we get the seeds. And from that, we grow gardens for the generations that follow us. This semester Locklear and I have given each other gifts that the other has never had; for me, she is my first Native student; for her, I am her first Native professor. We inhabit a unique cultural and academic situation that we felt was critical to capture.

This work focuses on the literature related to Native students and professors at predominantly White institutions (PWIs) and then specifically on the experiences and lives of Megan and I as Lumbee women and scholars, and the commonalities and differences therein, at our respective and shared institutions. We use the terms *Native, Native American, American Indian, Indian,* and *Indigenous* interchangeably when referring to the first peoples of the land now known as the United States, we also use tribal names, specifically *Lumbee,* when possible.

Being Native in the Academy

Native Students in Higher Education

Native American students currently make up approximately 1% of the undergraduate student population at universities in the United States and less than 1% of the graduate population (PNPI, 2019). Despite an increase in undergraduate- and graduate-level college enrollment by Native students from 2000 to 2010, Native enrollment dropped 31% between 2010 and 2017 (NCES, 2018). Though 60% of the general population attend college after high school, only 17% of Native American students enroll (Postsecondary National Policy Institute [PNPI], 2019). Additionally, for those who enroll, 41% obtain a bachelor's degree within 6 years (PNPI, 2019). Enrollment and persistence "remain concerns as Native students continue to fall below the national average," and these metrics are intensified and morphed by "[l]ow matriculation and campus climate . . . [f]eelings of not belonging . . . [a]cts of racism and/or perceived cultural differences" and can result in students unenrolling (Brayboy, Solyom, & Castagno, 2015, p. 158).

Native students who have lived in their tribal territories and communities for all or most of their lives also often experience deep feelings of incongruence between their home culture and university culture (Brayboy, Solyom, & Castagno, 2015). Students' tribal communities, which may be centered around notions of collaboration and mutual success, may be at odds with the individual-centric ideology of the academy, and they may find it difficult to give back to their own communities under these constraints (Brayboy, 2005; Brayboy, Solyom, & Castagno, 2015; Lundberg & Lowe, 2016; Waterman, 2007). Additionally, when students do not conform to these new standards, their professors may interpret their classroom performance negatively, which can subsequently impact their grades (Burk, 2007).

Native students are also faced with maintaining their Indianness, which we define simply as having ancestral ties to the continent now called North America, pre-colonization, *and* claiming and being claimed by a Native community, tribe, or nation. However, they are tasked with maintaining this Indianness in spaces that "often contradict what the media, larger society, and non-Native individuals hold for American Indian people" (Brayboy, 2004, p. 129). Sometimes, rather than committing to the exhausting effort that involves mitigating these identities, both real and perceived, American Indian students choose to use to their advantage the invisibility to which PWIs subject them (Brayboy, 2004). These students may choose to "make [themselves] less visible as a way to avoid romanticization, marginalization, and surveillance, while actively maintaining their sense of cultural identity or Indianness" (Brayboy, 2004, p. 130).

This invisibility, which many Indigenous students wield to their advantage, can often be protective regarding academic performance, as well. Research on preservice teachers by Brayboy and Maughan (2009) showed that Indigenous students were scored lower by their instructors when their lessons were framed from an Indigenous perspective; articulating their lessons from a dominant perspective provided better results. Cultural conflicts in the classroom arise due to the undervaluing of Indigenous ways of knowing, being, and learning. These experiences can intensify Indigenous students' feelings of unbelonging to their university and can result in them further isolating and distancing themselves from campus life (Lowe, 2005).

Native students also often report experiencing racism or microaggressions at their universities (Brayboy, 2015; Caplan & Ford, 2014). These experiences create even more conflictual feelings of cultural incongruence as students increasingly feel disconnected to and misaligned with university culture (Brayboy, 2015). In a study by Tachine, Cabrera, and Yellow Bird (2017), one student reported her peers making comments such as, "Wow, Native Americans have it so easy. They have everything handed to them—they're waited on hand and foot" (p. 797). This study also references experiences of Native students who were stereotyped based on their dialect and told, "You don't sound like a Native" (p. 796).

Lumbee students experience similar forms of linguistic microaggressions. Scott and Brown (2008) identified a Lumbee student who attended college away from home and said, "Some people here told me I didn't know my English and I need to learn it" (p. 509). The student was offended by the comment but made light of it. She stated that, though she does try to abide by mainstream English standards at school, "I feel like when I go back home, the country just comes back out in me somehow" (p. 509). Another student indicated feeling the necessity of code-switching, indicating that he "masked his dialect and became a part of the game of success" (p. 515). Others indicated having to repeat themselves multiple times to help others understand them, which was a source of consternation and embarrassment for them.

As a respite to these anti-Indigenous contexts, Native students also often have strong ties to "home" and maintain deep connections to their communities; they often travel back weekly and refer to this as "going home" (Lundberg & Lowe, 2016). However, in many college student development paradigms, family and home are considered "a detractor of success" (Lundberg & Lowe, 2016, p. 5). For Native students, though, this maintenance is positively correlated with their academic success and considered an asset and a strength (Guillory & Wolverton, 2008; Lundberg & Lowe, 2016). Additionally, Native students are uniquely and powerfully situated to "combine school knowledge and traditional knowledge in efforts to protect and to contribute to the power of [their] Native communities" (Salis Reyes, 2019, p. 606). Therefore, Indigenous students' frequent home-going is as purposeful as their coursework and perhaps even more critical. It remains critical, however, for Native students to maintain some semblance of a "home away from home" at their respective institutions. Relationships with peers who respect Native culture, Native friends, and staff support all contribute to this sense of belonging (Oxendine, 2015; Tachine, Cabrera, & Yellow Bird, 2017).

Native Doctoral Students For undergraduates and graduate students alike, a central theme emerges that plagues their time at the University—invisibility. Though American Indian undergraduate enrollment is low, 1%, doctoral enrollment is lower, 0.5% (National Center for Education Statistics [NCES], 2017). Out of the 1,500 universities in the United States that offer PhD programs, only 746 American Indian students received doctoral degrees in 2017 (NCES, 2017). Like undergraduates, Native doctoral students also have financial constraints, feel unsupported, and have a desire to give back to their tribal communities, despite universities providing little opportunities or pathways to do so (Brayboy, Solyom, & Castagno, 2015; Salis Reyes, 2019). Native doctoral students also often have competing responsibilities and report having to care for older family members more often than their non-Native peers (Limb, 2001).

Solutions for Native Student Success It is critical that universities adopt culturally responsive practices that produce greater alignment between Native students' tribal identities (Brayboy, Solyom, & Castagno, 2015). On-campus support, academic preparation, and financial support have been identified as integral to Native students' success (Guillory & Wolverton, 2008). Hernández-Avila (2003) outlined her personal experiences in the academy and her strategies for success, citing laughter, "dance, song, smudging, ceremony, play, family, community, art, writing" as "powerful antidotes[s]" (p. 242). She also notes that "the academy is a sickening place, but as Native scholars, we can create another kind of space" (p. 244). Diné scholar Shelly Lowe (2005) outlined several recommendations in an essay on helping Native students survive and thrive in the academy, including orienting Native students to campus life as well as to the local area, helping students feel like a part of the university family, providing them with a unique place to which they belong that houses Native faculty and staff, and supporting Native students' tribal identities.

Native Faculty in Higher Education

There is much research regarding the impacts of Native faculty on Native student success (Lowe, 2005; Tachine, Cabrera, & Yellow Bird, 2017; Tierney, 1995; Tippeconnic Fox, 2005). There is considerably less research, however, on the importance of representation for Native faculty. Native faculty currently make up 0.5% of university faculty positions (Walters et al., 2019). Kidwell (1990) notes the scarcity of Native faculty and staff nationwide and states that Native faculty often feel overburdened to create Native courses, to represent all Native people in any discussions of Native-related topics, and to be an expert in all Native-related content. This experience is not unique to Indigenous people; cultural taxation within the academy is common amongst the larger Black, Indigenous, and People of Color (BIPOC) faculty community (Guillaume & Apodaca, 2020; Joseph & Hirshfield, 2011). Stein (1996) found that many Native faculty believed that their colleagues assumed they were hired only because of their Native American identity, not because of their academic and professional merits. Native faculty also report experiencing racism, microaggressions, and isolation within the academy, which is further problematized by a lack of access to culturally relevant mentoring (Tippeconnic Fox, 2005; Walters et al., 2019). Walters et al. (2019) included the following excerpt of a poem from a Native female professor in their study of Native faculty in the academy:

> [I have] been counseled to end my activities in the community.
> I developed high blood pressure after taking this job.
> My husband wants me to quit *before they kill my spirit entirely.* (p. 622)

This professor felt that the academy had/has an eroding effect on her general well-being, that she was under constant departmental scrutiny and was viewed as "otherwise personally and professionally diminished," despite having secured national praise for teaching and service (p. 622).

Despite many obstacles and much defeat, Native faculty members often maintain strong connections to their homes and tribal communities much in the same way as Native students (Walters et al., 2019). These connections are often undervalued or viewed as superfluous by their non-Native peers but are protective and supportive for Native faculty (Hernández-Avila, 2003; Walters et al., 2019). Belk (2018) states:

> New professors of color are expected to do all sorts of work that seldom counts toward tenure. They must diversify the university with their mere presence, serve as role models for minority students, and represent alternative viewpoints on everything from the curriculum to university governance by serving on numerous committees. In essence, professors of color must solve the institution's diversity problem without earning recognition for the work. (p. 143)

Despite this labor Native and other marginalized faculty are both subject to and compelled by, like BIPOC students, BIPOC faculty have enacted methods of *survivance*, defined by Gerald Vizenor (1999) as "an active sense of presence, the continuance of Native stories, not a mere reaction, or a survivable name. Native survivance stories are renunciations of dominance, tragedy, and victimry" (p. vii). Native faculty do not exist simply as eternal victims of the academy, but their very existence within it is an act of resistance, visibility, and power (Walters et al., 2019).

Theoretical Framework—Tribal Critical Race Theory

Brayboy's (2005) Tribal Critical Race Theory (TribalCrit) is the framework guiding this work. Tenets of the theory include the following:

1. Colonization is endemic to society;
2. U.S. policies toward Indigenous peoples are rooted in imperialism, White supremacy, and a desire for material gain;
3. Indigenous peoples occupy a liminal space that accounts for both the political and racialized natures of our identities;
4. Indigenous peoples have a desire to obtain and forge tribal sovereignty, tribal autonomy, self-determination, and self-identification;
5. The concepts of culture, knowledge, and power take on new meaning when examined through an Indigenous lens;
6. Governmental policies and educational policies toward Indigenous peoples are intimately linked around the problematic goal of assimilation;
7. Tribal philosophies, beliefs, customs, traditions, and visions for the future are central to understanding the lived realities of Indigenous peoples, but they also illustrate the differences and adaptability among individuals and groups;
8. Stories are not separate from theory; they make up theory and are, therefore, real and legitimate sources of data and ways of being;
9. Theory and practice are connected in deep and explicit ways such that scholars must work towards social change. (Brayboy, 2005, pp. 429–430)

TribalCrit informs this work by underscoring the critical role colonization has played and continues to play in shaping American universities. Brayboy contends that our educational systems have been designed to assimilate Indigenous people; this claim is not ahistorical but is rooted in centuries-long attempts at dominating Indigenous peoples via Indian boarding schools and other measures (Caruthers, 2007; Gram, 2016; Lomawaima, 1993; Zalcman, 2016). This work exists as a countermeasure to this assimilationist practice.

This theory's focus on storytelling as a legitimate source of theory and data is fundamental. In her work on missing and murdered Indigenous women (MMIW), Sarah Deer (2015) notes "there is a kind of knowledge we gain from years of careful study" and "a kind of knowledge we gain from experiencing something, a visceral knowledge that can invoke the physical senses and the genius of memory" (p. 14). For Indigenous people in the academy, either as students or professors, these realities are often made invisible. Brayboy's (2005) tenet that "Indigenous peoples have a desire to obtain and forge . . . self-determination, and self-identification" (p. 430) is also central to this work due to our status as Indigenous within the academy; despite academia's constant pull toward assimilation, we demand different realities that affirm and reaffirm our Indigeneity.

Modes of Inquiry

This work is informed by Indigenous research methodologies that prioritize Indigenous people and are predicated upon Indigenous ways of knowing and being (Lambert, 2014). TribalCrit, as well as Critical Race Theory, similarly emphasize the power of storytelling and counterstorytelling (Brayboy, 2004; Iverson, 2007; Ladson-Billings & Tate, 1995). Iverson (2007) notes that "the university, through educational policy, conveys a whitewashed version that appears to be the only truth" (p. 604). We purport that certain truths, particularly Indigenous ones, are masked within higher education. If these stories are told, they have the power to usurp white supremacy's reign within the academy (Iverson, 2007). In this work, we prioritize ourselves and our own Indigenous voices in ways that the university has not and perhaps will not; we create spaces of power for ourselves with the power of our own research.

The present work focuses on my experiences as a Lumbee lecturer/professor and doctoral student (referred to in the Modes of Inquiry and Results sections, for clarity, as Hunt) and those of a Lumbee undergraduate social work student (Locklear). Hunt and Locklear met when Locklear enrolled in Hunt's course. The Lumbee lecturer (Hunt) is a 31-year-old female, and the Lumbee undergraduate (Locklear) is a 23-year-old female. Though Hunt and Locklear grew up in the same county of North Carolina and in the same tribal territory, their homes were in different tribal communities; thus, they have both similar and differing experiences with their respective Lumbee identities. Their paths to academia were also different based on their upbringing. All these similarities and differences are brought to this work.

This work is the compilation of two days of conversations with one another. In one sitting, Hunt asked Locklear more about her experiences both growing up in her Lumbee community and with the university. These questions included, but were not limited to: *Whoz ya people? What strengths do you bring as both a first-generation and as a Lumbee student? How is having a Lumbee professor different from having a non-Native professor?* and *Have you ever experienced imposter syndrome?* Locklear asked Hunt similar questions, including: *Whoz ya people? What is it like to be a Native woman in a doctoral program? How does it feel to teach a Lumbee student in a non-Native environment?* and *Being Lumbee, do you find it harder to live away from home?* Hunt and Locklear created their questions away from each other, but similar themes emerged between the two: connections to home/Lumbee identity, surviving in non-Native spaces, and experiences in the class shared as teacher and student. One question that was identical for both Hunt and Locklear was, *Whoz ya people?* Though the two women had discussed this before, both felt it was critical to begin the interview in this way. *Whoz ya people* (Who are your family?) is a common greeting among Lumbee people who are meeting for the first time or attempting to establish a connection between each other. It is "a way to establish a kinship connection and to understand where in the tribe's social life the person fits," according to Lumbee historian Malinda Maynor Lowery (2018, p. 6). Audra Simpson (2014) notes similar mechanisms of relationality among her Mohawk people:

> "Who are you?" There is always an answer with genealogic authority – "I am to you this way . . ."; "this is my family, this is my mother, this is my father"; "thus, I am known to you this way" . . . the webs of kinship have to be made material through dialogue and discourse. The authority for this dialogue rests in knowledge of another's family, whether the members are (entirely) from the community or not. "I know who you are." *Pointe finale.* We are done; we can proceed. (p. 9)

Therefore, *Whoz ya people?* is a way that Lumbee people relate to one another on a level that can be perplexing within Western education or American society with its respective emphases on *what you do* or *where you work* or *how well you do* or *how well you work*; we instead ask *who are you in relation to who I am and to who my people are?* This connectivity is not a Lumbee nor Mohawk phenomenon; it is a universally Indigenous concept, of establishing relation, identifying kinship, diminishing the *me*, and becoming the *we*. These questions and this Indigenous propensity for connection underlie our own research and our own questions for each other.

Analysis

All conversations were recorded and transcribed in their entirety. Transcripts were then coded for themes. Individual themes were derived from both conversations and used to construct overall meaning. The results and discussion were created from these co-constructed themes: the importance of family, being Lumbee in the academy, resistance and resilience, and the power of representation.

Results

Whoz Ya People: The Importance of Connection and Family for Lumbee Women

Both interviews began with the same question: *Whoz ya people?* Hunt and Locklear each answered this question, outlining specific family histories, telling of their grandparents, the communities they grew up in, the traumas and triumphs they have endured in those places. Home was critical to both Hunt and Locklear. Their homes are located in the same county—Robeson County, North Carolina—though in different communities therein. Both indicated traveling home significantly more often than their peers or colleagues. Locklear stated:

> I feel like it's a different experience for me when I go home too, because I feel like when I say I'm going home, it's like I'm literally going to a different place, like mentally, physically, going into a different mode of who I am. So, it's really like when I come back here, I put on the student, the adult, you know, that role of who I am. But when I go home, I'm just a daughter, a sister.

Locklear also indicated feeling simultaneously more relaxed and stronger at home, citing her strong influence in her family and over family decisions. This assuredness varies significantly from the uncertainty and ambivalence often accompanying academia. For Locklear, home is security.

Hunt also indicated a closeness to home is vital, citing regular trips home both while an undergraduate and now as a teacher and a doctoral student. She reminisced about these visits, stating:

> So, when I was at Duke [undergrad] . . . I was going home every single weekend . . . And my peers thought it was so strange that I was going home that often. I even knew people, friends whose families lived in Durham, and they only saw their family once a semester . . . And so, to me, their lifestyles were so bizarre cause I couldn't imagine not seeing my family . . . Like to me, that would just be completely not me living out who I really am. Going home was something that I just did regularly but then I realized that if I wanted to be successful, I couldn't go home as much. But also, if I wanted to be successful, I couldn't *not* go home at all. Going home was a part of my success.

For Hunt, there is a delicate balance between maintaining her grades at school and maintaining her connection to home that must be struck for her to find success; none can be maintained fully without the other.

In discussing the different socioeconomic barriers and crime rates within her tribal territory within the classroom, Hunt reported her students are often shocked by the violent stories they read or hear. To this, Locklear said: "But for us, that's home. It doesn't matter what would happen there, it would still be home to me. No matter, nothing, nothing could ever make that not be my home." For both Hunt and Locklear, home transcends space and circumstance; it is a place that they can always and will always go back to because it is central to their identities as Lumbee women and because it is where their families are.

Lumbee Identity in the Academy

Also salient for both women are their experiences of maintaining their Lumbee identities in universities that are non-Lumbee and often anti-Indigenous. Hunt stated,

> And so, you're in a whole different world where you really don't fit in all that well because the universities are not designed for us, they were really designed against us. And so, I think a lot of Lumbee students are struggling with *how do I stay Lumbee but also survive at this university?*

More specifically, Lumbee students, and Native students in the South in particular, often face a racial binary that allows only for White and Black identities, but never Indigenous ones (Lowery, 2010). Locklear stated,

> I just remember talking to Papa about it, and he was like, when you go to the city, there are only two races. You're either White or you're Black. So, if they don't know what you are, they're just gonna put anything on you.

Lumbee students resist these labels but often find it difficult not to buckle under the assimilatory pressures of the university. Though initially most Lumbee students are eager to share their Native identity with their non-Native counterparts in the academy, they soon face a barrage of insults and microaggressions that make disclosing their identities feel precarious and uncomfortable: *—Are you sure you're Native? How*

much Native are you? You look White/Black to me. Natives aren't Southern!
These realities force a disempowered silence onto students at a time
when their voice is most critical.

Lumbee people also possess a distinctive dialect that is complete with
its own verbiage and grammatical rules (Wolfram & Reaser, 2014). However, these dialects are often considered bad, broken, or "country" by
non-Lumbees (Wolfram, Adger, & Christian, 2007). Locklear noted the
following of her initial days at the university:

> Basically, everybody laughed as soon as I would speak, so nobody took
> me seriously, and then I kind of fell into that act, like nobody's taking
> me seriously. *So, I didn't take myself seriously sometimes.* Or I would just
> laugh and joke when really, sometimes, I would just be serious. Or some-
> times I would just have to prepare myself for the three-minute talk
> about my accent before I could actually say what I wanted to say.

Hunt echoed similar sentiments of frustrations with how her dialect
was perceived and the inevitable adaptations she made to avoid similar
run-ins, noting:

> I think it's a difficult process, and for me, that meant code-switching.
> So, I had to learn how to be Lumbee at home, but then when I get to
> school, I had to do a version of my voice that will be more accepted by
> non-Native people. So that's what I did then. Now I code-switch back
> and forth so effortlessly that I don't even think about it. I wish that I
> didn't, though. I wish that I didn't.

Though code-switching provided some immediate relief, its effects are
felt with sorrow. Through learning to code-switch effortlessly, Hunt now
feels that her dialect is weakening. She stated:

> A student the other day . . . they almost made me want to cry, cause
> she said she knew this Lumbee man. She was asking me if I knew
> him . . . And she's like, "Yeah, his accent was way stronger than
> yours though." And the way she said it was almost like "good job." But
> in my mind, I'm like, "God, I don't, I don't want that." You know, I don't
> want to, I don't want to lose my accent at all. And when I go home it
> comes back full force, but when I'm here I can hear myself sometimes
> and I'm like, "Oh my God, I've totally switched over and I didn't even
> realize it."

Therefore, in addition to struggles over maintaining their identities as Lumbee within spaces that demand otherwise, Hunt and Locklear experienced surveillance over the most intimate parts of their Indigenous selves, even down to the way they speak. These surveillances can often result in the unintentional severing of parts of themselves they want to keep but the university wants to erase.

Resistance and Resilience

Despite these barriers, Hunt and Locklear persist. They discussed the unique ways they resisted and were resilient to the challenges of university life. Locklear noted being a first-generation college student and her realization of these challenges:

> I always wanted to go to college. I just didn't know, like it was a whole systematic thing. *There's a reason why certain people don't go to college or they can't go.* I didn't realize all this stuff. So, as I'm learning, I think the first, the first mountain, I would say that I faced was my FAFSA and my mom did not know what to do. My grandma didn't know what to do and I was calling a bunch of 1-800 numbers trying to get help . . . And I just remember the look on my grandma's face. Like when she knew she couldn't help me, but she really wanted me to do this. It hurt me.

Locklear was soon disenchanted with the collegiate experience when she became ensnared by the dubious, bureaucratic, counterintuitive processes that accompany admission to and success in universities. Hunt expressed similar feelings, stating:

> I think I'm going to be the first Native American person to graduate from my program. I think. And I, I don't feel proud about that. I feel like that means the university has a big flaw. The fact they haven't graduated a Native person from my program ever, that doesn't make me feel proud of myself . . . It makes me feel like: "What is wrong with this university?" . . . And then a lot of times too, when we talk about people being the first in our family to graduate college, a lot of times they're the first who did, but they're also the first person who could, you know? I think about that a lot, like, OK, it's good that they did it, but there were all these barriers for their family members before them that made it impossible for them to go.

In reflecting on their own experiences in the academy, the two women spoke about their regrets, successes, as well as methods used to speak up about their Lumbee people. Hunt stated:

> People are never thinking about things from an Indigenous perspective. Even when they show statistics on poverty or on this or on that, they'll have Black, White, Hispanic, Asian, and then they'll never include, nobody will ever include American Indians. And so, I feel a lot of times in my undergrad program, I did not count at the university. Like in a paper I wrote, I was researching the number of Native professors in general. In one report they didn't even include our number but had an asterisk that meant: *American Indian rounds to zero* . . . how can I round to zero? So, that's how I kind of feel in my doctoral program. Like, I almost round to zero, but also, I feel like I make so much noise and I'm like, so, "Hey, well think about it like this, or like in the Lumbee community it's this." And so, it's like, *you're not going to round me to zero*, you're going to round me to at least one, I will at least be one. I'm not going to be nothing.

Both Lumbee women have developed powerful mindsets of resistance and resilience that continually propel them toward success despite academia's pull toward Indigenous erasure and invisibility.

This phenomenon, or rather, colonial structure, of erasure of Indigenous peoples, is not limited to academic spaces but is a part, if not the foundation, of Americana. Tuck and Yang (2012) note that settler-colonial societies have "multiple simultaneous and conflicting messages about Indigenous peoples, such as all Indians are dead, located in faraway reservations, that contemporary Indigenous people are less Indigenous than prior generations, and that all Americans are a 'little bit Indian'" (p. 9). This ideology serves to uphold settler colonialism by both erasing and dismissing the representation of Indigenous people in modern contexts, including media, governance, and schooling.

The Power and Responsibility of Representation

A final theme that emerged from these conversations was the power *and* responsibility of representation both for Hunt, teaching her first Lumbee student, and for Locklear, being taught by her first Lumbee professor. These experiences are complementary and critical. Locklear recalled her experiences in high school, where she had many Native women teachers; she remembers feeling they had taken care of her. Of her experiences in Hunt's classroom, she stated:

I got that same warm, familiar feeling that I had with my teachers in high school, but it was just like, I knew, I don't know how to explain it, but like I knew that I was gonna be OK in the class. Like I didn't feel nervous . . . I always do well in my classes, but it's always a nervousness. Like, how is the teacher going to be? How was her perspective? . . . But for that class I was like, I don't know. *I felt like I could take a deep breath.* Not saying like it's going to be easy. I knew I was going to learn and do the work, but I just knew I would be able to do it.

After taking the class, Locklear also noted a change in the classmates in her cohort. She experienced feeling *validated* in her Indianness in a way that she had not before; though her classmates had expressed doubts, disbelief, or ignorance when she spoke about her Lumbee identity, Hunt's presence "made it more real" and legitimated it. Though it is unfortunate that her classmates expressed reticence of her Indigenous identity prior to taking Hunt's class, Locklear notes that this speaks to the "power of Native professors."

Hunt noted similar feelings of her experience teaching her first Native and first Lumbee student; she said:

I was so excited . . . But I also was nervous because then I was like, OK, I gotta do more. More Indigenous content. I can't just do unlearning stereotypes this semester cause you wouldn't have those same stereotypes. I've had to go further . . . So I felt a lot of different emotions of excitement, but also . . . more responsibility.

Similarly, Locklear noted feeling greater responsibility because she wanted to represent herself well and did not want Hunt to "feel ashamed" of her. Locklear also noted that observing Hunt's pursuit of a doctoral degree was personally inspiring and confirmatory to her; Hunt's pursuit made her own pursuit seem all the more possible and "familiar." Others pursuing similar degrees from other communities or ethnic backgrounds did not provide that same degree of familiarity. That is the power only a Native professor can bring to a Native student.

Discussion

Our (referring to Hunt and Locklear) connection to home, our struggles in the academy, our acts of resilience and resistance, and finally, the power of representation that we mutually provided to each other—these ties reinforce the dual importance of Native students and Native professors in the academy. There is a symbiosis between the two, an understanding, particularly in PWIs, that helps both feel seen in contexts that strive to make us unseen. We both experienced confused looks from our peers over our connectivity to home. In his work on TribalCrit, Brayboy (2005) notes, "For many Indigenous people, culture is rooted to lands on which they live as well as to their ancestors who lived on those lands before them" (p. 434). For us, our identity as Lumbee people is intrinsically rooted in our homeplace; we cannot function as scholars without a regular connection to it. This is unintelligible to many but intuitive for us. Brayboy also notes that "concepts of culture, knowledge, and power take on new meaning when examined through an Indigenous lens" (p. 429). Lumbee culture, knowledge, and power are not tethered to our usefulness to the academy, nor our ability to assimilate within it, but are instead derived from our ability to connect with one another, maintain relationships, learn from our elders, and teach our youth.

TribalCrit particularly emphasizes colonialism's entrenchment in society; Brayboy (2005) notes, "the goal, sometimes explicit, sometimes implicit, of interactions between the dominant U.S. society and American Indians has been to change ('colonize' or 'civilize') us to be more like those who hold power in the dominant society" (p. 430). As Lumbee women in the academy, we are well acquainted with these unfortunate truths. We both have endured experiences that have pushed and pulled us toward the settler-colonial goal of Indigenous assimilation or erasure, toward adopting the traits of the dominant group and forsaking our own Indigenous ones. And while erasure seeks to remove or make invisible, assimilation seeks to replace, to change beyond recognition. We reject both. As Lumbee women in Southern contexts that demand ascription to the racial binary, we have also found that within the academy, we occupy spaces that seek to racialize us and do not account for our Indigenous identities. Our Indigenousness seems foreign, peculiar even, to our non-Indigenous peers, who are accustomed to being spoon-fed narratives of Natives in the past, leathered and feathered, living in tipis on the plains and surrounded by buffalo. Hunt et al. (2020) detail the experiences of Lumbee students in urban schools who were often plagued by questions and comments like: "Well, you don't look Indian. You look like a White girl. Do you speak Indian? Do you live in a teepee? Do you have running water? How do you have the clothes that you have?" (p. 12). Brayboy (2005) notes that "viable images have instead been replaced with fixed images from the past of what American Indians once were," or perhaps never were (p. 431). Lumbee historian Malinda Maynor Lowery (2018) notes the stories told about American Indians within modern media (textbooks, television, news) "sound dissonant, out of sync" with the stories we tell of ourselves (p. 2).

As Lumbee women and scholars, we have used the tools in our arsenal to resist and rebuff the colonial forces at play in our lives and to tell our own stories of ourselves. TribalCrit maintains that Indigenous people desire to maintain self-determination and self-identification. Our acts of defiance, of visibility, and of mere presence within the academy push us toward sovereignty. But at what point in our lives as Native women and scholars is everything, not just a constant test or struggle or barrier? Therefore, though we celebrate our tenacity, we also recognize the exhaustion the university brings to Indigenous women.

Finally, we acknowledge the beauty of representation. Scholars have long indicated the importance of representation for students in having teachers and professors who look like them. But that importance is mutual. Professors, too, want to teach students from their own communities; not exclusively, but certainly not sporadically, either. The power of seeing another Indigenous person in your classroom—as a student or as a professor—is powerful. It signifies solidarity and removes the possibility of being alone in a space that was not designed for even one of us, much less two. Additionally, there is power in numbers. Institutional change cannot be achieved without it. But beyond that, beyond making the academy better, beyond this free labor that both Native students and faculty often provide, there necessitates a space of *home*, of kinship, of *whoz ya people?* for Lumbee students and faculty to feel belonging, safety, and liberation. This is the essence of this work. Not that we must change for the academy, labor for it, or love it, but that it works instead to provide us the resources we need to create community away from home.

The mutual responsibility, respect, and pride shared between a Native student and Native teacher, particularly within spaces where their numbers might *round to zero*, is critical. Though we provide no numerical data, we give our stories, and Brayboy notes that "stories are not separate from theory; they make up theory and are, therefore, real and legitimate sources of data and ways of being" (p. 430). Our stories make real the importance of representation.

Conclusion

Though the academy is rooted in colonialism, it can be wielded as a powerful tool for Indigenous scholars seeking to bring back institutional knowledge to their own communities. Though Indigenous scholars do not leave the academy unscathed in the process, and though we find our own conceptions of our Indigenous identity pushed to our perceived limits, we learn instead that they are limitless. Many of the stories we shared as a part of this work centered around the indomitable will of our families, how they persevered despite insurmountable odds and made sacrifices for us to be where we are today. Our own work in the academy has taught us of another indomitable will, not just of our mothers and grandmothers, but of ourselves. Burkhart (2004) notes of Indigenous identity, "We are, therefore I am" (p. 25). We Indigenous people define ourselves in relation to each other; we are not a collective of individuals, but rather a people forever connecting, whether by *whoz ya people?*, by education, by resilience, or by our ancestral need to be connected to each other.

Dr. Brittany Danielle Hunt is a member of the Lumbee Tribe of North Carolina. She is currently a postdoctoral research associate at Duke University. She is a graduate of Duke University and the University of North Carolina at Chapel Hill.

Megan Locklear is a member of the Lumbee Tribe of North Carolina. She is currently working as a social worker in Chicago.

REFERENCES

Belk, A. G. (2018). Review of written/unwritten: Diversity and the hidden truths of tenure. *Journal of Political Science Education, 14*(1), 141–144. https://doi.org/10.1080/15512169.2017.1366327

Brayboy, B. M. J. (2004). Hiding in the Ivy: American Indian students and visibility in elite educational settings. *Harvard Educational Review, 74*(2), 125–152. https://doi.org/10.17763/haer.74.2.x141415v38360mg4

Brayboy, B. M. J. (2005). Toward a Tribal critical race theory in education. *The Urban Review, 37*(5), 425–446. https://doi.org/10.1007/s11256-005-0018-y

Brayboy, B. M. J. (2015). Indigenous peoples in the racial battle land. In K. Fasching-Varner, K. A. Albert, R. W. Mitchell, & C. M. Allen (Eds.), *Racial battle fatigue in higher education* (pp. 45–58). Rowman and Littlefield.

Brayboy, B. M. J., & Maughan, E. (2009). Indigenous knowledges and the story of the bean. *Harvard Educational Review, 79*(1), 1–21. https://doi.org/10.17763/haer.79.1.l0u6435086352229

Brayboy, B. M. J., Solyom, J., & Castagno, A. E. (2015). Indigenous peoples in higher education. *Journal of American Indian Education, 54*(1), 154–186. https://www.jstor.org/stable/10.5749/jamerindieduc.54.1.0154

Burk, N. M. (2007). Conceptualizing American Indian/Alaska Native college students' classroom experiences: Negotiating cultural identity between faculty and students. *Journal of American Indian Education, 46*(2), 1–18. https://www.jstor.org/stable/24398566

Burkhart, B. Y. (2004). What Coyote and Thales can teach us: An outline of American Indian epistemology. In A. Waters (Ed.), *American Indian thought: Philosophical essays* (pp. 15–26). Blackwell Publishing.

Caplan, P., & Ford, J. (2014). The voices of diversity: What students of diverse races/ethnicities and both sexes tell us about their college experiences and their perceptions about their institutions' progress toward diversity. *Aporia, 6*(3), 30–69. https://diversity.missouristate.edu/Assets/diversity/Voices_of_Diversity_Project_Caplan_Ford.pdf

Caruthers, L. (2007). The soil of silence: Deconstructing socio-cultural and historical processes that have influenced schooling for First Nations People and African Americans. *American Educational History Journal, 34*(1/2), 303–313. https://go.gale.com/ps/i.do?id=GALE%7CA252849364&sid=googleScholar&v=2.1&it=r&linkaccess=abs&issn=15350584&p=AONE&sw=w&userGroupName=anon%7E2c734bc9

Deer, S. (2015). *The beginning and end of rape: Confronting sexual violence in Native America*. University of Minnesota Press.

Gram, J. R. (2016). Acting out assimilation: Playing Indian and becoming American in the federal Indian boarding schools. *American Indian Quarterly, 40*(3), 251–273. https://www.muse.jhu.edu/article/633377

Guillaume, R. O., & Apodaca, E. C. (2020). Early career faculty of color and promotion and tenure: the intersection of advancement in the academy and cultural taxation. *Race, Ethnicity and Education*, 1–18. https://doi.org/10.1080/13613324.2020.1718084

Guillory, R., & Wolverton, M. (2008). It's about family: Native American student persistence in higher education. *Journal of Higher Education, 79*(1), 58–87. https://www.jstor.org/stable/25144650

Hernández-Avila, I. (2003). Thoughts on surviving as Native scholars in the academy. *American Indian Quarterly, 27*(1/2), 240–248. https://doi.org/10.1353/aiq.2004.0034

Hunt, B., Locklear, L., Bullard, C., & Pacheco, C. (2020). "Do you live in a teepee? Do you have running water?": The harrowing experiences of American Indians in North Carolina's urban public K-12 schools. *The Urban Review*. https://doi.org/10.1007/s11256-020-00563-1

Institutional Research Analytics. (2020). *Fact book: Enrollment summary dashboard*. UNC Charlotte, Division of Academic Affairs. https://ir-analytics.uncc.edu/tableau/fact-book-enrollment-summary-dashboard

Iverson, S. V. (2007). Camouflaging power and privilege: A critical race analysis of university diversity policies. *Educational Administration Quarterly, 43*(5), 586–611. https://doi.org/10.1177/0013161X07307794

Joseph, T. D., & Hirshfield, L. E. (2011). "Why don't you get somebody new to do it?' Race and cultural taxation in the academy. *Ethnic and Racial Studies, 34*(1), 121–141. https://doi.org/10.1080/01419870.2010.496489

Kidwell, C. (1990). Indian professionals in academe: Demand and burnout. In *Opening the Montana Pipeline. Proceedings from the American Indian Higher Education in the Nineties Conference, Bozeman, MT*. Tribal College Press.

Ladson-Billings, G., & Tate, W. E., IV (1995). Toward a critical race theory of education. *Teachers College Record, 97*(1), 47–68. https://www.unco.edu/education-behavioral-sciences/pdf/TowardaCRTEduca.pdf

Lambert, L. (2014). *Research for Indigenous survival: Indigenous research methodologies in the behavioral sciences*. Salish Kootenai College Press.

Limb, G. E. (2001). Educating for practice: A profile of American Indian graduate social work students. *Journal of Ethnic and Cultural Diversity in Social Work, 10*(4), 43–62. https://doi.org/10.1300/J051v10n04_03

Lomawaima, K. T. (1993). Domesticity in the federal Indian schools: The power of authority over mind and body. *American Ethnologist, 20*(2), 227–240. https://www.jstor.org/stable/645643

Lowe, S. C. (2005). This is who I am: Experiences of Native American students. In M. J. Tippeconnic Fox, S. C. Lowe, & G. S. McClellan (Eds.), *Serving Native American students* (pp. 33–40). Jossey-Bass.

Lowery, M. M. (2010). *Lumbee Indians in the Jim Crow South: Race, identity, and the making of a nation*. University of North Carolina Press.

Lowery, M. M. (2018). *The Lumbee Indians: An American struggle*. University of North Carolina Press.

Lumbee Tribe of North Carolina (Lumbee Tribe). (2016). *History and culture*. https://www.lumbeetribe.com/history-and-culture

Lundberg, C., & Lowe, S. (2016). Faculty as contributors to learning for Native American students. *Journal of College Student Development, 57*(1), 3–17. https://doi.org/10.1353/csd.2016.0003

National Center for Education Statistics (NCES). (2017). *Doctor's degrees conferred by postsecondary institutions, by race/ethnicity and sex of student: Selected years, 1976-77 through 2016-17*. https://nces.ed.gov/programs/digest/d18/tables/dt18_324.20.asp

National Center for Education Statistics (NCES). (2018). *The condition of education: Undergraduate enrollment*. https://nces.ed.gov/programs/coe/indicator_cha.asp

Office of Institutional Research. (2009). *Full-time teaching faculty by rank, sex, and race, Fall 2009, Table VII-5*. https://ir.uncc.edu/sites/ir.uncc.edu/files/media/factbook/fb09/fb09085.pdf

Oxendine, S. (2015). Examining the impact of institutional integration and cultural integrity on belonging to predict intention to persist for Native American students at non-Native colleges and universities (Doctoral dissertation). *ProQuest Dissertations and Theses database*. https://libres.uncg.edu/ir/uncg/f/Oxendine_uncg_0154D_11637.pdf

Postsecondary National Policy Institute (PNPI). (2019). *Factsheets: Native American students*. https://pnpi.org/native-american-students/

Salis Reyes, N. (2019). "What am I doing to be a good ancestor?": An Indigenized phenomenology of giving back among Native college graduates. *American Educational Research Journal, 56*(3), 603–637. https://doi.org/10.3102/0002831218807180

Scott, C., & Brown, K. (2008). Rising above my raisin'?: Using heuristic inquiry to explore the effects of the Lumbee dialect on ethnic identity development. *American Indian Quarterly*, *32*(4), 485–521. https://doi.org/10.1353/aiq.0.0029

Simpson, A. (2014). *Mohawk interruptus: Political life across the borders of settler states.* Duke University Press.

Stein, W. (1996). The survival of American Indian faculty. In C. Turner, M. Garcia, A. Nora, and L. I. Rendón (Eds.), *Racial and ethnic diversity in higher education* (pp. 390–397). Pearson Custom Publishing.

Tachine, A., Cabrera, N., & Yellow Bird, E. (2017). Home away from home: Native American students' sense of belonging during their first year in college. *The Journal of Higher Education*, *88*(5), 785–807. https://doi.org/10.1080/00221546.2016.1257322

Tierney, W. (1995). Addressing failure: Factors affecting Native American college retention. *Journal of Navajo Education*, *13*(1), 3–7. https://eric.ed.gov/?id=EJ541697

Tippeconnic Fox, M. J. (2005). Voices from within: Native American faculty and staff on campus. *New Directions for Student Services*, *2005*, 109, 49–59. https://doi.org/10.1002/ss.153

Tuck, E., & Yang, K. W. (2012). Decolonization is not a metaphor. *Decolonization: Indigeneity, Education and Society*, *1*(1): 1–40. https://clas.osu.edu/sites/clas.osu.edu/files/Tuck%20and%20Yang%202012%20Decolonization%20is%20not%20a%20metaphor.pdf

University of North Carolina (UNC) Charlotte. (2019). *2019 progress report for UNC Charlotte plan for campus diversity, access, and inclusion.* https://diversity.uncc.edu/sites/diversity.uncc.edu/files/media/2019%20Progress%20Report%20of%20Campus%20Plan%20for%20Diversity-Access-Inclusion%20UNCC.pdf

Vizenor, G. R. (1999). *Manifest manners: Narratives on post Indian survivance.* University of Nebraska.

Walters, K. L., Maliszewski Lukszo, C., Evans-Campbell, T., Burciaga Valdez, R., & Zambrana, R. E. (2019). "Before they kill my spirit entirely": Insights into the lived experiences of American Indian Alaska Native faculty at research universities. *Race, Ethnicity and Education*, *22*(5), 610–633. https://doi.org/10.1080/13613324.2019.1579182

Waterman, S. (2007). A complex path to Haudenosaunee degree completion. *Journal of American Indian Education*, *46*(1), 20–40. https://www.jstor.org/stable/24398461

Wolfram, W., Adger, C. T., & Christian, D. (2007). *Dialects in schools and communities.* Lawrence Erlbaum Associates.

Wolfram, W., & Reaser, J. (2014). *Talkin' Tar Heel: How our voices tell the story of North Carolina.* The University of North Carolina Press.

Zalcman, D. (2016). "Kill the Indian, save the man": On the painful legacy of Canada's residential schools. *World Policy Journal*, *33*(3), 72–85. https://doi.org/10.1215/07402775-3713029

The Five-Factor Model of Indigenous Studies: A Quantitative Content Analysis of Postsecondary Indigenous Studies Websites in Canada, the United States, Australia, and New Zealand

ADAM T. MURRY, TYARA MARCHAND, EMILY WANG, AND DANIEL VOTH

Indigenous Studies (IS) is a multidisciplinary academic discipline chartered to offer more than just an education about Indigenous peoples. Indigenous Studies is a fought-for space on campus to properly represent the perspectives, processes, and communities of Indigenous peoples, for the benefit of Indigenous communities, organizations, and interests. Unfortunately, the extent to which IS fulfills its mission is ambiguous due to the wide variation in IS program composition, the broad scope of the discipline's topical foci, and the lack of parameters or core ingredients that distinguish it from other disciplines. In this article, we describe the process and results of a content analysis of IS websites in the United States, Canada, Australia, and New Zealand. The goal of this study was to identify the major features of IS internationally and to show how IS programs vary in their embodiment of those major features. After an extensive coding process, we ran an exploratory factor analysis on the quantitative codings to derive a five-factor model of IS. Accordingly, IS included (1) Indigenous methodologies, (2) Indigenous community member involvement, (3) Indigenous Ways of Knowing and Doing, (4) Indigenous languages, and (5) Indigenous student community. How much these factors were emphasized depended on the country, institution type, and level of degree offered, controlling for website complexity and aesthetics. Our findings show that there is common ground across IS programs internationally, according to their websites, but that some countries (e.g., Canada), institution types (e.g., tribal colleges), and degree programs (e.g., undergraduate) reflect these factors more than others.

IN 2017 THE University of Calgary launched "ii'tah'poh'to'p," a university-wide initiative dedicated to partnerships with neighboring First Nations and taking actionable steps toward decolonization, Indigenization, and reconciliation. The initiative developed through relationships between the University of Calgary's senior administration, faculty, and Elders from surrounding First Nations, particularly Provost Dru Marshall, faculty member Jacqueline Ottmann (Anishinaabe), and Elder Reg Crowshoe (Piikani) of the Blackfoot Confederacy. The initiative, referred to as the Indigenous Strategy, involved two years of planning and consultation and built upon the momentum of Canada's Truth and Reconciliation Commission's report and Calls to Action (Truth and Reconciliation Commission [TRC], 2015). Elder Andy Black Water (Kainai) transferred the name "ii'taa'poh'to'p," meaning a place "to rejuvenate and re-energize while on a journey" (University of Calgary, 2017).

The initiative spurred activities at every level, including curriculum reviews, cluster hires, new course offerings, renovated spaces, dedicated staff, revised policies, heightened accountability, and seven committees to monitor progress and inform processes. The buzz around Indigenization brought attention to our International Indigenous Studies program, which, like many IS programs, lacked dedicated staff, faculty, and infrastructure. In the summer of 2019 Daniel Voth took the position of our IS program's director, and in the months following, worked to form a governance committee, review the course offerings, create new courses, hire staff and faculty, and maintain the program's ongoing activities.

By December 2019 the governance committee was called upon to discuss future directions for IS at our university. Our vision was supposed to guide which currently available classes were defined as our core courses, which had to be created if they did not exist, who was going to teach those classes, and who would need to be recruited and hired to teach them if our faculty did not have adequate coverage. The governance committee comprised four IS staff and faculty and five Indigenous faculty in the faculty of arts. Committee members represented a diverse range of specializations, including political science, English, art and art history, medical anthropology, and organizational psychology (Adam T. Murry). Notably, none of us had a PhD in IS, which, in our experience, is not surprising for IS programs. Indigenous Studies regularly recruits faculty and cross-lists course offerings from a range of disciplines, including linguistics, literature, history, anthropology, environmental science, political science, health science, social science, law, and business, among others. As such, it was difficult to make decisions about how to embody the unifying aspects of IS or how to distinguish ourselves from other programs. Murry and Voth decided to conduct a study on the defining characteristics of IS as a discipline. Thanks to the diligent work of Tyara Marchand and Emily Wang, and the Indigenous Student Access Program (University of Calgary, n.d.a) and Program for Undergraduate Research Experience (University of Calgary, n.d.b) programs that helped fund them, we present an empirical model of IS for the consideration of other IS programs, their stakeholders, and non-IS programs with shared objectives.

Background

Indigenous Studies is an academic discipline dedicated to teaching and research on the culture, history, literature, language, art, politics, sciences, and contemporary affairs of Indigenous peoples. Indigenous Studies programs are multidisciplinary, combining their own courses with those from an array of departments (e.g., linguistics, archeology, cultural studies, and geography), with much variation in what a particular program will emphasize. Majoring or minoring in IS prepares students to work in sectors relevant to Indigenous communities (e.g., public policy, education, law, environmental studies) and purportedly centers Indigenous perspectives on these areas more so than anywhere else on campus.

Like other ethnic and distinguished group studies (e.g., Black Studies, Gender Studies), IS was born in response to political and student organizations' fights for representation in college and university settings during and following the Civil Rights Era. As described by Gay (1983):

> Whereas other activists could speak passionately and from personal knowledge about racist practices in employment and housing, many of the students could not. But they did know from personal experience what it was like to spend 12 or more years in school without ever seeing their ethnic peoples and experiences portrayed except in stereotypic, derogatory ways. . . . [A]s the idea grew to conceptual maturity, multicultural education came to mean both content and process, curriculum and pedagogy, ideology and policy. (pp. 561, 562)

Unlike other ethnic studies, the meaning of representation and control over content in IS has special implications due to Indigenous peoples' unique political status and relationship with federal governments. For one, in the United States, Canada, New Zealand, and Australia, Indigenous peoples are recognized in national constitutions (e.g., The U.S.

Constitution), legislation (e.g., Canada's Indian Act of 1876; Te Ture Whenua Maori Act of 1993), and legal definitions (e.g., tribal enrollment in the United States or band status in Canada) to be distinct nations and original inhabitants of the land. In the United States, Canada, and New Zealand, this relationship is codified in treaties, which simultaneously worked to disenfranchise Indigenous peoples of their territories and recognize their nationhood and pre-established occupancy (Boldt & Long, 1984). Second, all these countries implemented similar colonial programs, which sought to assimilate, marginalize, or eradicate their Indigenous populations (e.g., relocation, reserve/reservation systems, enfranchisement [loss of tribal status], termination [of treaty relationship], residential/boarding/day schools, criminalization of identity, sterilization, and removal of children from family members of cultural-ethnic heritage, among others). The combined effect of this legacy has been a continued effort to resist assimilation through the reclamation of sovereignty and self-determination (see charters of the Assembly of First Nations [Assembly of First Nations, n.d.] and the National Congress of American Indians [n.d.]; United Nations Declaration on the Rights of Indigenous Peoples [UNDRIP, United Nations General Assembly, 2007]). In Indigenous education, representation and control over content are not simply another movement toward a more inclusive society, but rather a demonstration of Indigenous sovereignty, the freedom to maintain continuity with one's culture, history, and people, and, in some locations, the fulfillment of long-standing treaty relationships between Indigenous nations and the nation-state.

Working from this depiction, IS should not only be a discipline where students can learn about Indigenous peoples, similar to the way one would learn about ancient Rome. Indigenous Studies should also be a way that Indigenous students can obtain a college education that is in alignment with and inclusive of their Indigenous orientations and perspectives, and non-Indigenous people can experience those orientations and learn those perspectives. In this sense, IS should be the epicenter of Indigenization efforts on campus and a model for all curricular attempts to integrate content that is important to Indigenous communities' self-determination, cultural revitalization, voice, and students' preparation to contribute to those things.

Perhaps due to IS's existence being the result of broader social movements for justice and representation (Gay, 1983; Nakata 2004), what defines the essential elements of IS, or what it is supposed to be, has not been well articulated (Andersen, 2009; Barney, 2014; Champagne, 2007). Australia is the exception, largely due to the work of library scientist Martin Nakata [Torres Strait Islander] (2003, 2006, 2011, 2013; Martin et al., 2017; Nakata et al., 2012, 2014) and his network (Barney, Shannon, & Nakata, 2014; Day et al., 2015) and perhaps influenced by local educational-political dynamics that forced disciplinary articulation. Nakata et al. (2012) delineate the conceptual framework of IS as being grounded in *decolonization, Indigenous Knowledge pathways,* and *the restoration of Indigenous Ways of Knowing and Doing.* Although the gold standard of whether this is occurring relies on local, community-based appraisals of IS programs (e.g., tribal/band leadership, prominent figures, ceremonial leaders, Knowledge Keepers, Elders), other disciplines that are working to integrate Indigenous perspectives and knowledges corroborate the agendas outlined by Nakata et al. (2012) Examples include decolonization in education generally (Battiste, 2017; Battiste, Bell, & Findlay, 2002; Thaman, 2003), pedagogy specifically (Garcia & Shirley, 2012; Pelletier & Gercken, 2006), in land rights (Corntassel, 2012), and social science (Steinman, 2015). Similarly, integrating Indigenous Ways of Knowing has been defended in education (Barnhart & Kawagley, 2005), forest conservation (Charnley, Fischer, & Jones, 2007), conservation biology (Drew & Henne, 2006), ecology (Gagnon & Berteaux, 2009), wildlife conservation (Huntington, 2000, 2002), and public health (Simonds & Christopher, 2013).

Despite the calls for IS to represent an Indigenous intellectual presence on campus, to date there has been no empirical demonstration that IS resembles what scholars articulated or for what activists hoped. This study attempts to fill that gap by quantitatively evaluating the way IS programs describe themselves across four countries. The results will allow stakeholders of IS programs to gauge whether and how much their local program aligns with attributes proclaimed across the discipline, whether their own interests in IS match what IS purports to offer, and whether the major features of IS's self-description aligns with the discipline for what Indigenous scholars and students fought. Stakeholders include IS students, their families, scholars, curriculum developers, university administrators and leadership, and Indigenous communities that fund and/or benefit from students with degrees in IS, or the local, city, municipality, state, province, Band, Tribal, and federal agencies that hire IS graduates.

To evaluate the core features of IS we content- and factor-analyzed IS program websites across Canada, the United States, Australia, and New Zealand. We chose these countries because of the shared colonial experience of their Indigenous peoples (Archibald, 2006; Bramley et al., 2004; Cooke et al., 2007; Cornell, 2006; Gray & Beresford, 2008; Hunter

& Harvey, 2002; McIntyre et al., 2017; Reyhner & Singh, 2010; Smylie et al., 2010) and their overlapping security (e.g., Five Eyes/UKUSA agreement), economic and political values (Bell & Vucetic, 2019). Indigenous Studies websites were used because they are publicly available, provide information that organizations wish to convey about their culture and work environment (Braddy, Meade, & Kroustalis, 2006), and advertise the positive qualities a program wishes to present about itself to stakeholders (e.g., branding pro-diversity workplaces; Jonsen et al., 2021). In other words, websites provide a snapshot of how IS wants to present itself. Since this type of evaluation of IS is the first of its kind, we posed two exploratory research questions:

1. What are the major features of Indigenous Studies, as portrayed through their university-based websites?
2. How do those major features differ, depending on program characteristics?

Positionality and Methodology

While this study follows conventional standards in quantitative research, we contend that our efforts still represent an Indigenous methodology. As described by Māori methodologist Linda Tuhiwai Smith (2012), Indigenous methodologies can be grounded in Indigenous philosophical assumptions (e.g., epistemologies; see Kovach, 2009) and paradigms (e.g., relationalism; see Wilson, 2008), or grounded in Western methods for the purpose of furthering Indigenous self-determination, decolonization, and Indigenization. This is similar to what Ray (2012) referred to as Indigenous convergence versus strategic methods, the latter of which this study belongs. Regardless of the specific method, Indigenous methodologies often endorse reflexive or positionality statements from the authors of research (Kovach, 2009; Wilson, 2008; Walter & Andersen, 2016). This practice is in alignment with introductory protocols in many Indigenous cultures to situate who is speaking, which helps to build relationships between the readers and the authors and allows the audience to contextualize the message, the message sender, and the perspectives they represent.

The first author, Adam T. Murry, is of Ukrainian, Irish, and Apache descent and works as an assistant professor in the department of psychology, where he has created courses in qualitative research, Indigenous research methods, and Indigenous psychology. He serves as a committee member on the IS governance committee at the University of Calgary and is heavily invested in Indigenization efforts in Western institutions (e.g., Murry et al., 2021; Murry & James, 2021; Murry, James, & Drown, 2013; Murry & Wiley, 2017). The second author, Tyara Marchand, is an avid member of the Okanagan Indian band near Vernon, British Columbia (sitting as co-chair of the Okanagan Indian Band youth leadership council), an honors graduate in anthropology, specializing in maternal-child wellness, and, as of fall 2021, a medical school student. The third author, Emily Wang, is an accounting major who has worked with Indigenous communities across British Columbia and Alberta in various capacities: for example, serving as a youth leader with the National Youth Reconciliation Initiative, among other roles. She started law school in the fall of 2021. The fourth author, Daniel Voth, is Métis from the Métis Nation of the Red River Valley, an associate professor of political science, and the director of IS and its governance committee at the University of Calgary.

As a team we represent a range of perspectives, spanning occupational role, education level, discipline, age, gender, Indigenous heritage, tribal affiliation, and nationality, to name a few. The diversity among the team helped us to think about our topic through multiple angles; however, there are ways in which our perspectives align and influence our interpretation. For one, we are all in agreement that higher education, despite its faults, can be a vehicle for improved health and well-being for many Indigenous individuals and communities. However, institutions of higher learning need to invest in, and be held accountable to, top-down (e.g., institution-led) and bottom-up (Indigenous-led) strategies to increase the safety, relevance, and access of higher education to Indigenous communities and their members. We believe that efforts to integrate Indigenous culture (i.e., Indigenization), eliminate vestiges of racism and ethnocentrism (i.e., decolonization), and build Indigenous-Settler relationships based on mutual respect and integrity (i.e., reconciliation) will increase representation, retention, and self-determination, but we recognize that some websites are closer to those objectives than others. We are hoping the work we have done to support our own IS program will serve the translational purpose of making Indigenization comprehensible and actionable to sites at all points on the spectrum of Indigenization readiness. Finally, it should be noted that we all work with and are regularly exposed to websites and online content, and, as such, have working assumptions of what a good website should entail in terms of aesthetics, functionality, usability, and communication. It is possible these assumptions do not hold across

Indigenous populations, particularly since Indigenous communities are described as being "disconnected" with multiple barriers to things like broadband access and internet infrastructure (e.g., Government Accountability Office, 2018; Smillie-Adjarkwa, 2005). We still think investigations into the use and meanings of Indigenous content online are worthwhile, however, since research also shows that Indigenous internet use exceeds that of the non-Indigenous population when access is wireless (Morris & Meinrath, 2009; Showalter et al., 2019) and that Indigenous youth regularly use the internet for social media, information sharing, entertainment, updates about news, sports, and current events, and health information (Rushing & Stephens, 2011).

Methods

Sample Eligibility for website inclusion was determined by the college/university having (1) an undergraduate, major and/or minor, or graduate, master's or doctoral, IS program with a website that was (2) written in English. Exclusion criteria included (3) the college/university having enrollment less than 2,000 students, and (4) being a technical or religious institution. Not all colleges and universities have an IS program, but we found them to be least likely among small, specialty institutions. These exclusion criteria were selected to help reduce the number of irrelevant searches in our initial screen. Due to their relevance to our topic, tribal, band, or otherwise Indigenous community-operated colleges were included regardless of student enrollment size as long they met our other inclusion criteria.

Out of 332 college and university IS websites scanned, 76% met eligibility criteria for coding (N=238). The resultant sample contained 174 U.S. institutions (73%), 32 Canadian institutions (13.4%), 26 Australian institutions (11%), and six New Zealand institutions (2.5%). The vast majority were publicly funded institutions (N=200; 84%), although private (N=21; 8.8%) and tribal (N=16; 6.8%) colleges were present in the sample. Indigenous Studies programs were offered as minors (N=191; 80.5%), bachelor's degree majors (N=105; 44%), honors (N=49; 20.5%), 2-year/associate's degrees (N=29; 12%), master's-only (N=19; 8%), and master's/PhD (N=19; 8%). Only 21 (8.8%) offered a topical specialization according to their website.

Procedure Eligible websites were content analyzed between May and July of 2020. The entire IS website was used for coding purposes, including clicking on links, tabs, and multiple pages. Our primary focus was on program descriptions, charters/About pages, philosophies, and goals and outcomes; we also attended to program characteristics (e.g., major/minor) and attributes of the website design (e.g., usability and the amount of information/pages/tabs/links). A coding process delineated by Krippendorff (1989, 2018) was used on the content available on each website, including main pages (e.g., home, history, about, news, and faculty pages), bulletin boards, announcements, newsletters, events pages, testimonial pages, links to faculty biographies, and recruitment pages.

To code eligible websites, we developed a codebook based on (1) a literature review of scholarly discussion about Indigenous Studies and (2) consultation with the IS governance committee. First, Marchand and Wang separately conducted literature reviews on the scholarly discussion about IS. The search yielded 28 peer-reviewed sources (see Appendix). Marchand and Wang extracted constructs that scholars argued characterized or should characterize IS and then met to consolidate those constructs into codes, that is, labels representing units of meaning (Krippendorf, 1989, 2018). After consolidation, we presented the codes and definitions to the IS governance committee to refine or add codes related to goals of IS from their perspectives (e.g., employment opportunities). After input was compiled, we created a codebook, and coders scanned every IS program website in Canada, the United States, Australia, and New Zealand that met the above-stated criteria. Coding involved the enumeration of a code's presence or absence.

Instruments The codebook contained 13 codes on IS program characteristics (e.g., degree type), 27 codes for constructs of theoretical interest (e.g., mention of Indigenous epistemologies; see Table 1), and three codes on website quality (e.g., usability). Code scales were nominal (e.g., country, institution type), binary (e.g., theoretical constructs), ordinal (e.g., website quality), or continuous (e.g., units required). To ensure mutual understanding of the descriptive and operationalized constructs, three randomly selected websites were coded by both coders at the beginning (week 1 of 10), middle (week 4), and end (week 10) of the coding process. Coders agreed 88% of the time at time 1 (Kappa [κ] = .75), 100% of the time at time 2 (κ = 1), and 91% of the time at time 3 (κ = .83). All percent agreements and κ statistics were impressive by conventional standards (i.e., substantial to almost perfect agreement; McHugh, 2012).

Analysis To answer research question 1, we ran an exploratory factor analysis (EFA) on website ratings on our 27 codes of theoretical interest using maximum likelihood estimation on the correlation matrices with varimax rotation. Factors with eigenvalues over 1 were

Table 1 List of Coded Constructs in Mean Rank Order With Standard Deviation (SD) and Sample Size (N)

Coded construct of interest for Indigenous Studies	N	Mean (0-1)	SD
Present-orientation	238	0.81	0.40
Cultural aspects	238	0.81	0.40
Multidisciplinary focus	238	0.66	0.48
Indigenous student council	237	0.63	0.48
Indigenous self-determination	238	0.61	0.49
Indigeneity (opportunities to practice culture)	238	0.53	0.50
International focus	238	0.47	0.50
Employability	238	0.45	0.50
Indigenous research	238	0.45	0.50
Indigenous language classes	238	0.44	0.50
Locally based traditional teaching	238	0.44	0.50
Indigenous nomenclature (traditional names for local Bands/Tribes)	238	0.41	0.49
Indigenous epistemologies	238	0.39	0.49
Indigenous community member involvement in teaching	238	0.32	0.47
Employment opportunities	238	0.30	0.46
Indigenous faculty	238	0.29	0.46
Indigenous pedagogies	238	0.28	0.45
Indigenous methodologies	238	0.27	0.44
Holism	238	0.27	0.44
Diversity	238	0.24	0.43
Decolonization	238	0.22	0.42
Cultural interface between Indigenous/ Western	238	0.19	0.40
Land-based learning	237	0.19	0.39
Intergenerational focus	237	0.16	0.37
Traditional territorial land acknowledgments	238	0.16	0.37
Reconciliation	238	0.12	0.33
Cultural competence	238	0.04	0.20
Valid N (listwise)	235		

Note. Mean scale is from 0 (absent) to 1 (present) across Indigenous Studies websites internationally.

labeled and interpreted as the major features of IS programs. To answer research question 2, we ran multivariate analyses of covariance (MANCOVA) with mean composite scores based on our EFA as dependent variables and program characteristics as independent variables. Included program characteristics were (1) country (i.e., Canada, United States, Australia, New Zealand), (2) institution type (i.e., public, private, tribal), and presence of an IS (3) undergraduate degree (i.e., none vs. AA/BA) or (4) graduate program (none vs. master's/PhD). To control for confounds, website quality metrics (i.e., complexity/content amount and aesthetics/ease of use ratings) were entered as covariates.

Results

Fundamental Characteristics of Indigenous Studies

After dropping 11 coded items that cross-loaded on multiple factors or failed to load sufficiently on any factor, the final EFA revealed five factors, explained 62% of the remaining 16 items' total variance. The five underlying factors of IS were (1) *Indigenous methodologies* (i [item]= 4; $M = 0.28$), (2) *Indigenous community member involvement* ($i = 3$; $M = 0.28$), (3) *Indigenous Ways of Knowing and Doing* ($i = 3$; $M = 0.28$), (4) *Indigenous languages* ($I = 3$; $M = 0.43$), (5) *Indigenous student presence* ($i = 3$; $M = 0.66$). Within each factor, items' internal consistency was acceptable or near acceptable for all but Indigenous student presence ($>= .70$; John & Benet-Martinez, 2000; see Table 2). These factors represent the major features of IS according to IS website depictions across Canada, the United States, Australia, and New Zealand. The identification of these five elements answers research question 1 by empirically defining the major features of IS according to IS programs' self-descriptions (see Table 2).

Variation by Program Characteristics

The multivariate test, which looked at the effect of program characteristics across all five IS factors simultaneously, identified statistically significant relationships for country ($p < .001$), institution type ($p < .001$), and the presence of an undergraduate program in IS ($p = .001$), controlling for website complexity and aesthetics. The presence of a graduate program did not predict differences across the five-factor model of IS ($p = .13$). Our covariates, website complexity ($p < .001$) and website aesthetics ($p < .001$), had a significant and strong effect on the presence of our five-factor model. Effect sizes were in the medium range, with the

Factors

Code/construct	1 Indigenous methods	2 Community involvement	3 Ways of knowing	4 Indigenous languages	5 Indigenous students
Indigenous methodologies	.74				
Indigenous research	.61				
Decolonization	.50				
Cross-cultural interface	.48				
Indigenous involvement		.68			
Indigenous faculty		.59			
Diversity		.51			
Indigenous pedagogies			.67		
Indigenous epistemologies			.56		
Intergenerational focus			.53		
Nomenclature (Indigenous words)				.67	
Locally based teaching				.52	
Indigenous languages taught				.43	
Indigenous student council					.71
Cultural aspects					.45
Indigeneity					.44
Total variance explained	32%	9.36%	8.28%	7.11%	6.29%
Eigenvalue	4.96	1.50	1.33	1.14	1.01
Mean	0.28	0.28	0.28	0.43	0.66
SD	0.33	0.36	0.35	0.38	0.34
Cronbach's alpha	0.74	0.70	0.69	0.66	0.56

Note. Table reports total variance explained by each factor along with their eigenvalues, items' average and standard deviation (SD), and measure of internal consistency (i.e., Cronbach's alpha). Sample adequacy was sufficient according to the Kaiser-Meyer-Olkin (KMO) estimate (KMO = .85). Only factor loadings >= .40 shown here.

Table 3 Multivariate Analysis of Covariance (MANCOVA)
Omnibus Results Across Dependent Variables

Independent variables	F	df	Error df	p	η^2	β
Country	5.52	15	678	<.001**	.11	.86
Institution type	3.80	10	450	<.001**	.08	.99
Undergraduate IS degree	4.43	5	224	.001*	.09	.97
Graduate IS degree	1.72	5	224	.13	.04	.59
Website complexity[†]	5.53	5	224	<.001**	.11	.99
Website aesthetics[†]	8.46	5	224	<.001**	.16	>.99

Note. F = multivariate F-statistic, Pillai's trace; df = degrees of freedom; *Error df* = error degrees of freedom; p = likelihood of difference by chance; η^2 = partial eta-squared effect size; β = statistical power; [†]model covariates; *statistical significance at p < .05; **statistical significance at p < .001

exception of website aesthetics, which had a large effect (Cohen, 1988; see Table 3). These results show that our five-factor model of IS varies by country, institution type, whether an IS program has an undergraduate degree, beyond the effects of websites' aesthetic appeal or amount of content. Statistically significant multivariate tests permit us to inspect the univariate relationships between country, institutional type, and the presence of an undergraduate degree on each of our five factors of IS.

Country By far the most ubiquitous effect was by country, where countries differed significantly on all five factors of IS: (1) Indigenous methodologies (p < .001), (2) Indigenous community involvement (p < .001), (3) Indigenous Ways of Knowing and Doing (p < .001), (4) Indigenous languages (p < .001), and (5) active Indigenous study body (p = .03). Pairwise tests, with Bonferroni corrections for multiple tests, showed that IS websites in Canada were more likely to describe Indigenous methodologies, community involvement, and Ways of Knowing/Doing than in the United States or Australia. Australian IS websites were less likely to use or showcase Indigenous languages compared to Canada, the United States, and New Zealand. Finally, the United States reported more Indigenous student activities than Canada (see Table 4 and Figure 1).

Institutional Type Univariate tests showed institutional type effects IS websites' descriptions of Indigenous methodologies and languages (p < .001). Private colleges' IS websites were more likely to mention Indigenous methodologies, research, decolonization, and cross-cultural interfacing, and tribal colleges' IS websites were more likely to reference

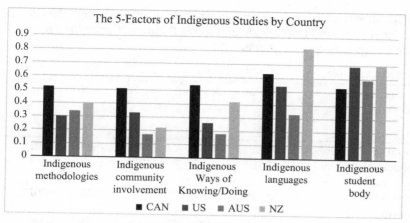

The 5-Factors of Indigenous Studies by Country

■ CAN   ■ US   ■ AUS   ■ NZ

Figure 1. The Five-Factor Model of Indigenous Studies by country, controlling for website usability and aesthetics (N=238).

Indigenous language courses, use Indigenous words and phrases on their website, and reference locally based teachings (see Table 4).

Undergraduate Degree Program Whether an IS program offered undergraduate degrees influenced what appeared on their website ($p = .002$). Indigenous Studies programs with undergraduate degrees refer to Indigenous Ways of Knowing (i.e., epistemologies) and Doing (i.e., pedagogies) on their websites more than those that do not. Similarly, Indigenous language courses and use are featured more on IS websites when they also offer an undergraduate degree (see Table 4).

Supplemental Analysis A question was raised by our reviewer whether a university/college's proximity to Indigenous lands/territories would affect the degree to which our five-factor model of IS showed up on IS websites. We calculated the driving distance from each university to the closest reserve/reservation's band/tribal office. Unfortunately, we were not able to calculate distances for Hawaii, New Zealand, or Australia using this standard due to differences in land allotments, land definitions, or points of reference. In the remaining sample of U.S. and Canadian institutions (N=197), proximity to Indigenous lands correlated only with IS websites' mention of Indigenous Ways of Knowing and Doing ($r = .19$, $p = .008$). When proximity to Indigenous land/territory was added to the previously described MANCOVA, no changes in statistical significance or mean rank were observed between the United States and Canada, although, as a covariate, proximity was significantly related to our five factors in the multivariate test.

Table 4 Univariate Tests Comparing Our Five-Factor Model of IS by Country, Institutional Type, and Undergraduate Degree Program, Controlling for Website Complexity and Aesthetics

Independent variables	CAN	US	AUS	NZ	p	η^2
Dependent variables (scale 0–1)	N = 32	N = 174	N = 26	N = 6		
Country						
Indigenous methodologies	0.52[a,b]	0.30[a]	0.34[b]	0.40	<.001**	.08
Indigenous community involvement	0.51[a,b]	0.33[a]	0.17[b]	0.22	<.001**	.09
Indigenous Ways of Knowing/Doing	0.54[a,b]	0.26[a]	0.18[b]	0.42	<.001**	.14
Indigenous languages	0.63[a]	0.54[b]	0.33[a,b,c]	0.82[c]	<.001**	.08
Indigenous student body	0.53[a]	0.69[a]	0.59	0.70	.03*	.04

Institution type	Public	Private	Tribal		p	η^2
	N = 201	N = 21	N = 16			
Indigenous methodologies	0.36[a]	0.51[a]	0.30		.02*	.03
Indigenous community involvement	0.29	0.26	0.38		.43	.007
Indigenous Ways of Knowing/ Doing	0.30	0.30	0.45		.15	.02
Indigenous languages	0.44[a]	0.42[b]	0.89[a,b]		<.001**	.10
Indigenous student body	0.63	0.63	0.63		.999	<.001

Undergraduate IS degree	Yes	No			p	η^2
	N = 128	N = 110				
Indigenous methodologies	0.43	0.35			.06	.02
Indigenous community involvement	0.31	0.31			.96	<.001
Indigenous Ways of Knowing/ Doing	0.43[a]	0.27[a]			<.001**	.06
Indigenous languages	0.66[a]	0.50[a]			.002*	.04
Indigenous student body	0.64	0.61			.57	.001

Note. Superscripts ([a,b,c]) are used to denote significant differences according to Bonferroni corrected pairwise tests; * univariate statistical significance at $p < .05$; ** univariate statistical significance at $p < .001$; η^2 = partial eta-squared effect size.

Validity Check: Website Content and Course Outlines

Although our study was about how Indigenous Studies is represented in websites, a logical next question is whether website content conveys in-class practices. As a check for predictive validity, up to six course outlines (i.e., syllabi) were pulled from IS websites whenever they were publicly accessible. Of the 238 IS websites, only 18 had course outlines that were publicly accessible (N=18). Of those 18, 56% were from Australian universities (N=10). From the 18 websites, 92 course outlines were retrieved (12 websites provided six course outlines, 33% had less than six posted).

Course outlines were rated according to the five IS dimensions identified previously (see Table 2), and then course outline ratings were averaged *within* the university. Ratings were on a scale from 1 to 5, with "5" meaning more prominent mention of that IS dimension (e.g., see Table 5). We ran partial correlations, where website scores on the five dimensions were correlated with course outline ratings on the five dimensions. To correct for the fact that some IS websites had (1) less course outlines available, (2) fewer pages of content, and (3) generally less appealing or functional design, we controlled for (1) the number of course outlines available (1 to 6), (2) website complexity (e.g., number of pages, scale 1 to 7), and (3) website aesthetics (i.e., subjective standard, scale 1 to 7; $p < .05$). Due to the low sample size, we used bootstrapping with 1,000 samplings.

Across the five underlying dimensions that define IS, only the Indigenous Studies departments whose website claims to use Indigenous methods correlated with its presence in course outlines ($r = .57$, $p = .03$), controlling for the number of course outlines accessible and website complexity and aesthetics. Interestingly, if an IS website claimed use of Indigenous Ways of Knowing and Doing, this also correlated with Indigenous methodologies on course outlines ($r = .62$, $p = .01$). Indigenous websites' use of Indigenous language was related to Indigenous community member involvement in course outlines ($r = .58$, $p = .02$), and website claims to community involvement were marginally related to Indigenous student community presence on course outlines ($r = .46$, $p = .08$). Otherwise, website claims to Indigenous community involvement, Ways of Knowing and Doing, language use, and student community presence did not correlate with those practices in-class, according to course outline content ($p > .05$).

These results suggest that what appears on an IS website does not necessarily translate to the classroom, even after controlling for

Table 5 Factor Definitions and Examples From Indigenous Studies Websites

Factor name	Definition	Website example
Indigenous Methodologies	Research is based on the interests of Indigenous peoples and uses Indigenous teachings to guide their work. It can be conducted by non-Indigenous individuals as long as they are equal partners in the work with Indigenous peoples.	"As a community of learners, we connect and honour the academic rigor and Indigenous perspectives through activist research, creative production, and community engagement." (https://www.sfu.ca/indg/ about/people.html)
Indigenous Language	The use of labels that Indigenous peoples choose to identify with and the inclusion of Indigenous languages in the program.	"An eclectic selection of new and traditional elements including kapa haka, nga toango puoro, and creative technologies delivered by quality academics who are fluent in Maori." (https://www.waikato.ac. nz/study/subjects/maori -and-indigenous-studies)
Indigenous Student Community	Indigenous students are provided cultural, peer, and educational support. The quality of being Indigenous with a focus on kinship, land, and self-government. This involves creating space to share, display, and celebrate Indigenous ways of life.	"The center for American Studies is a home away from home where students can study, participate in student organization meetings, relax with friends, and seek assistance from an advisor or tutor." (https://www.bhsu.edu/ Academics/Math-Social -Sciences/American -Indian-Studies)

Indigenous Ways of Knowing and Doing	The method and practice of teaching that includes traditional ways of knowing. Indigenous knowledge pathways tend to be in contrast to Western knowledge.	"Following the Mamiwinin-mowin (Algonquin language) concept of aditawazi nisoditadiwin, or walking in two worlds, Carleton's Indigenous Studies program blends traditional academic instruction with Indigenous approaches to teaching." (https://admissions.carleton.ca/programs/indigenous-studies/)
Indigenous Involvement	Indigenous peoples being involved in Indigenous studies curriculum development and faculty.	"All students have the opportunity to enrich their learning by participating in field trips, circle learning, interaction with Elders, Sto:lo cultural teachings, and special guest lectures." (https://www.ufv.ca/indigenous-studies/program/ba-indigenous-studies/)

website quality. The few exceptions are noteworthy given that most IS programs often cross-list courses from other departments and faculties with little to no control over what or how they teach. However, since only 7.5% of our sample of universities had course outlines accessible to perform this check, these results should be considered preliminary and not used to make judgments about program activities.

Discussion

The aim of this investigation was to (1) quantitatively define the core or fundamental elements of Indigenous Studies (IS), as they are described by IS program websites, and (2) describe how those elements vary by program characteristics like geography or degree offered. Our content and factor analyses revealed five major ingredients of IS that held across academic program websites in the United States, Canada, New Zealand, and Australia. These ingredients included (1) Indigenous research and methodologies, (2) the involvement of Indigenous people in the instruction, (3) Indigenous epistemologies and pedagogies, (4) the use of and course offerings for Indigenous languages, and (5) an active Indigenous student body.

We also explored the extent to which our five-factor model of IS held across websites by country, institutional type, and degree offerings. We found that IS websites in Canada posted the most content on Indigenous methodologies, community involvement, and Indigenous Ways of Knowing and Doing. The United States was most likely to boast an active student body. Australia was least likely to showcase Indigenous languages and language use. Indigenous Studies programs at private colleges promoted Indigenous methodologies more than public or band/tribal colleges, while IS program websites at band/tribal colleges led in the use of Indigenous languages. Surprisingly, offering a graduate degree (master's/PhD) in IS did not impact their websites' coverage our five-factor model, but offering an undergraduate degree (associate's/bachelor's) increased descriptions of Indigenous Ways of Knowing and Doing and teaching/using Indigenous languages.

Implications

The findings of this study have implications for research and theory on IS as a discipline. Probably our biggest contribution was to move what has been more than two decades of discourse and case study about IS into a rigorous, quantitative empirical investigation. As Champagne (2007) wrote, IS "should be capable of generating theory, forming empirical research, making generalizations, commenting policy, and supporting the goals and values of [Indigenous] nations" (p. 353). We believe our study blends Indigenous creativity and perspective with empirical rigor.

A second implication of our study comes from the five-factor model of IS. Defining IS has been a reoccurring issue for the discipline (Andersen, 2009; Barney, 2014; Champagne, 2007), and we helped to assess its identity through its online self-presentation. Interestingly, our five-factor model did not contain specific topics, per se, but rather topical *domains* and types of Indigenous community involvement, leaving room for translation into local contexts. An intuitive example is with our factor on Indigenous languages. From our framework, one would expect IS programs to integrate Indigenous language. However, from our framework we would not expect all IS programs to offer courses in the same Indigenous language. Rather, it is reasonable to expect those courses to emphasize traditional languages spoken in or around the region in which the university is based. While the five factors are in some ways reductionist, the expressions and implementations are as varied and diverse as the populations who engage with them.

Despite the structure we have added, a third implication is our findings' confirmatory contribution. That is, we found what others have been saying for years. For example, the IS literature is ripe with arguments for Indigenous and decolonizing methodologies (Andersen & O'Brien, 2017; Battiste, 2017; Smith, Tuck, & Yang, 2019), Indigenous community involvement (Augustus, 2015; Fredericks, 2009; Nakata, 2006), Indigenous Ways of Knowing (i.e., epistemologies) and Doing (i.e., pedagogies) in education (Cross-Townsend, 2011; Fry, 2018; McGloin & Carlson, 2013; Nakata et al., 2012), the use of Indigenous language (Giacon & Simpson, 2012; Warrior, 2008), and the importance of a supportive Indigenous student community (Barney, 2013; Brayboy, 2004; Jackson, Smith, & Hill, 2003). It is our hope that reflecting their good work in statistical form will help translate those ideas to middle-of-the-road audiences who are more open-minded to research than Indigenous advocacy.

Applications

Our findings have potential applications for program directors, students, national/international associations, and Indigenous communities. Most obviously, our results can inform IS program website design to make sure it is keeping up with disciplinary trends. However, insomuch as these web-based IS trends reflect real and important perspectives, our results help to provide concrete examples of Indigenization. For example, to honor Indigenous methodologies, Simon Fraser University's IS website (retrieved December 2020) states that, "As a community of learners, we connect and honor academic rigor and Indigenous perspectives through activist research, creative production, and community engagement." The University of British Columbia's IS website opens with

> We would like to acknowledge that First Nations and Indigenous Studies and the University of British Columbia are located on the traditional, ancestral, and unceded territory of the Musqueam people. We thank the Musqueam Nation for its hospitality and support of our work.

To show their commitment to Indigenous Ways of Knowing and Doing, Carleton University's website (retrieved 2020) describes: "Following the *Mamiwininmowin* (Algonquin language) concept of *aditawazi nisoditadiwin*, or walking in two worlds, Carleton's Indigenous Studies program blends traditional academic instruction with Indigenous approaches to teaching." Finally, in support of the Indigenous student community, Black Hills State University's website claims that (retrieved December 2020): "The center for American Indian studies is a home away from home where students can study, participate in student organization meetings, relax with friends, and seek assistance from an advisor or tutor."

The five-factor model has uses beyond online communications. For example, students could use our model as a guide for evaluating programs. Similarly, program coordinators could use our model as an assessment tool of their program structure and resources. Should a program be found lacking in core content (e.g., Indigenous methodologies, languages), opportunities (e.g., cultural participation), structural integration (e.g., community member teachers and staff, community liaisons, and partnerships), and community (e.g., student body), assuming they want those things, our model could serve as a template to direct attention. With each level of assessment, decisions regarding recruitment and hiring (e.g., Indigenous faculty), teaching (e.g., Indigenous centered pedagogy), curriculum (e.g., methodologies), resources (e.g., smudge room), organizational practices (e.g., budget allocation to support IS [Loyer, Vanderwerff, & Bowler, 2017], flexibility paying Knowledge Keepers for teaching regardless of formal education), and community building can be directed according to need. For example, the role and importance of Elders in postsecondary education have been investigated and found to be an important resource for culturally sensitive education and transmitting sacred Indigenous Knowledge in a respectful manner (Anonson et al., 2014). Where resources or supports are lacking, directors might use this information to appeal to their department heads, deans, provosts, or other administration. Given the low average rates of community involvement depicted on IS websites, we, in fact, strongly encourage IS leads to do so.

National and international associations of IS (e.g., Native American Indigenous Studies Association; World Indigenous Peoples' Conference on Education) might apply our results to assist in categorizing research/applied activities for purposes of funding, recognition, or conference program listings. If research methodologies and pedagogies are distinct, as they were here, then perhaps conference submissions should be vetted so that there is an equal share of presentations addressing each. Associations that target undergraduates from certain countries may want to include content from our model for recruitment purposes.

Finally, Indigenous communities may apply our results to evaluate IS or other college programs with an Indigenous emphasis. Indigenous communities often provide support for Indigenous students on- and off-reserve to go to college (e.g., Community Futures Treaty 7). Indigenous communities might critically consider what type of education students are receiving. If members from Indigenous communities (e.g., parents, educators, leaders) endorse our five-factor model of IS, or any of its parts, as desirable end goals of the discipline or education in general, then perhaps those constituencies support or encourage students to pursue disciplines where those things are available. On the flip side, it is possible that IS has grown to cater more to non-Indigenous students seeking out Indigenous perspectives than to Indigenous students to become equipped to serve their communities. For instance, it was interesting that although employment-related topics appeared on websites often, they were not connected to the underlying factors of IS. If community needs and vision for IS differ from the five factors, IS will need to reconsider its identity, or at least how to distinguish IS's disciplinary identity from its educational priorities.

Limitations

This study was unique in its approach to quantitatively define IS, to contain a sample that nearly eclipses the population of interest, and to examine an academic discipline according to criteria named by Indigenous scholars. That said, there were several limitations.

The first limitation is related to what we can infer about the aspirations of IS through its online brand. As we demonstrated with our validity check, we cannot make judgments about what happens in-class or within-program based on our website data, with few exceptions (e.g., the use of Indigenous methodologies). While this does not detract from the goal of our study to understand how IS defines itself through publicly facing online content, one would hope that the more an IS website portrays elements of our five-factor model, the more those elements would show up in the program. That this was not the case in our validation check indicates that website development and course content remain separate entities with different drivers and constraints (e.g., IT resources versus Indigenization efforts). This was expected, in part, since IS programs' common practice of cross-listing courses from other departments means they would have less control over those courses' commitments and pedagogies.

A few limitations arose when determining institutions to include in the content analysis. Websites displayed in anything other than English were not included, preventing any inferences on schools with courses taught in other languages (e.g., in French). Additionally, eligible institutions were required to have a distinct minor or major degree option. This excluded schools that offered an Indigenous-focused stream within a separate program of study (e.g., education, social work). This decision was made because we sought to understand IS specifically in terms of its own self-description, and we reasoned that Indigenous streams within other disciplines would not be beholden to represent the interests of IS. This does not imply that Indigenization efforts in other disciplines do not advance Indigenous self-determination efforts or that their integration of Indigenous community and content is not important. Future research should evaluate whether our five-factor model shows up in streams in other disciplines.

Information on how schools allocate their resources to their websites or to their IS programs was not available. As such, some schools that we would expect to score high on our five-factor model did not, solely due to low-content websites. This was particularly relevant for tribal colleges, who tended to have websites with less content that were more difficult to use, possibly due to financial limitations (Fox, 2006). Although we controlled for this statistically in our comparative analyses, in practice a program that fully embodies our model might be invisible online. Second, even if an IS program website scored well on our five-factor model, it is not an indication that the university in which the program is housed supports it, nor that the courses affiliated with the program follow the lead of the IS program website (see Validity Check). While we contend that our five-factor model of IS represents meaningful ways IS distinguishes itself as a discipline, we recognize that programs do not always have control over their websites, the amount of content or pages allowed, or their functionality. Even where a particular program's website ranked high on our five factors, it is possible that this is due to overlapping university/college agendas or the availability of IT resources rather than the program offerings. This is an important caveat before extrapolating from a website to a program.

A few limitations were practical in nature. For example, this report involves data collected up to the end of August 2020. The information this work is based on does not include any changes or updates to institution websites or course outlines since data collection was completed.

This is of particular interest to us since our IS program's website was revamped after our analysis had concluded, and even borrowed from the knowledge we produced in its conceptualization. It is unknown how IS program website ratings from other institutions were affected by this timeline. Indigenous Studies website representation also heavily favored public institutions in the United States. Program websites at tribal colleges and in New Zealand had high mean rates of our five-factor model but failed to reach significance, likely because of small sample sizes.

A final limitation was the measurement of Indigenous student community. It was typically difficult to determine whether an institution offered a Native Student Center/Alliance/Council because many program sites did not highlight these resources. To make sure we did not neglect their presence, we searched through the general institution's web pages, but the burden of these additional searches likely impact how well we were able to assess their presence. This may have been the cause of the low alpha coefficient for this subscale.

Future Directions

Future research should follow up on our calls to investigate whether Indigenous constituencies, both traditional and contemporary, reserve and urban, individual and community, as well as IS students and faculty endorse our five IS factors. Provided local stakeholders agree with the five-factor model, future research should assess the utility of our model as a diagnostic tool for Indigenized higher education contexts. Such a tool could highlight areas of excellence or in need of improvement. For example, an institution that scored low on Indigenous involvement may consider hiring more Indigenous faculty or introducing Elders into their teaching staff, while a program that scored lower on Indigenous methods or pedagogies may need to seek out teaching resources, experts, and faculty.

A second avenue of future work could involve the concurrent validity of our five-factor model of IS. For example, one might correlate scores on our five factors with institutional resource allocation and program support. An institution that values diversity and diversity retention may invest more time and financial resources into its IS program or highlighting the Indigenous student community. This could be in the form of state-of-the-art Native center facilities (e.g., Portland State or Northern Arizona University) or the creation of modern and aesthetically pleasing website design.

In addition to a symbol of university values and practices, future research should unpack the meaning behind online/website presence within the university setting for Indigenous peoples. In an increasingly online world, Indigenous representation and self-determination are wrapped up with whether institutions give space to Indigenous peoples and their programs and how that space is regulated. Considering access and control over online platforms as a type of power-sharing, future research should build on our results by facilitating discussions around how IS programs and other on-campus Indigenous constituencies are being integrated or excluded from decision-making (Fredericks, 2009). Activists may see online space as a contested space where attention should be devoted. In this regard, it would be helpful to identify exemplars of such power-sharing in the university setting to see if and how it impacts online portrayals.

Third, research should look beyond websites to actual practice. While our five-factor model of IS provides parameters for an otherwise broad discipline, the five buckets we identified are also quite broad. It is expected that differences and similarities will surface across IS programs and that there are contextually moderated lessons to be learned in each domain. For example, tribally based IS programs did not differ significantly from nontribal IS programs, except for language use, despite our expectation that they would excel. This may be because tribal colleges and universities are funded by the tribal communities themselves (Pavel, Ingelbret, & Banks, 2009) and have limited resources to dedicate to websites, or they may not view online presentation as fundamental to their program's success. Word of mouth or other nonwebsite marketing strategies could be in effect, making website aesthetics and complexity irrelevant indicators of their programs' quality. Similarly, cultural integration and community involvement are probably more safely taken for granted in tribal colleges so that online resources are better allocated toward promoting local interests, like matriculation/transfer or employment. Future research should survey tribal colleges/universities to assess the five-factor model of IS and how important website presentation is to their institution's local community.

Last, a comprehensive survey asking postsecondary students about exposure to the elements identified in our five-factor model of IS should be investigated. Student outcomes such as sense of belonging, positive self-concept, community and self-esteem, motivation to learn, bicultural identity, course performance, grade point average, and others may be associated with higher or lower fulfillment of these factors. Indigenous Studies programs could be ranked by how much they embody each factor, and those scores could be correlated with student outcomes. Another direction might utilize qualitative methods to ascertain faculty, student, and community member perspectives around our five factors, perhaps from different countries, institutions, or degree types. This could help to unpack the factors according to local context, appraise whether the model overall or its parts are worthwhile (Carey & Prince, 2015; Nakata, 2006), or what their outcomes are perceived to be.

Conclusion

This study helped to define a discipline of symbolic and practical significance to Indigenous peoples and their allies in higher education. We showed that IS has a set of internationally shared characteristics and that IS programs vary in how well they embody those characteristics. Our hope is that the discipline grows in concept and resources as we work to live out Indigenous Ways of Being, Knowing, and Doing in all the places we reside.

Adam T. Murry is assistant professor of Indigenous psychology at the University of Calgary, where he runs the Indigenous Organizations' and Communities' Research lab. His research is committed to partnerships with Indigenous organizations and programs and involves the use of mixed-methods to assist Indigenous agendas within factors such as employment, health care, mentorship, allyship, and education.

Tyara Marchand has a degree in anthropology and is in her first year at the Cumming School of Medicine in pursuit of an MD degree. She is of Okanagan ancestry and has been working alongside Dr. Murry on a multitude of projects with a focus on Indigenous Studies and Indigenous Primary Health.

Emily Wang is in her third year at the Haskayne School of Business and will be attending law school in Fall 2021. Over the past few years, Emily has worked with Indigenous communities across Canada using art to bridge connections. Emily works under Dr. Murry in his research lab.

Daniel Voth is associate professor in the Department of Political Science at the University of Calgary and the Director of the International Indigenous Studies Program. He is Métis from the Métis Nation of Red River Valley. His research has been published in Canadian Journal of Political Science, University of Toronto Law Journal, Native American and Indigenous Studies Journal, and Canadian Journal of Undergraduate Research.

APPENDIX

Article list for code source	Location
Aberdeen, L., Carter, J., Grogan, J., & Hollinsworth, D. (2013). Rocking the foundations: The struggle for effective Indigenous Studies in Australian higher education. *Higher Education Review, 45*(3), 36–55.	Australia
Andersen, C., & O'Brien, J. M. (Eds.). (2016). *Sources and methods in Indigenous studies.* Taylor & Francis.	International
Andersen, C. (2009). Critical Indigenous studies: From difference to density. *Cultural Studies Review, 15*(2), 80–100.	Canada
Augustus, C. (2015). Knowledge liaisons: Negotiating multiple pedagogies in global Indigenous Studies courses. *Canadian Journal of Higher Education, 45*(4), 1–17.	Canada
Nakata, M. (2006). Australian Indigenous studies: A question of discipline. *The Australian Journal of Anthropology, 17*(3), 265–275.	Australia
Barney, K. (2014). A discussion with Sandy O'Sullivan about key issues for the Australian Indigenous Studies Learning and Teaching Network. *The Australian Journal of Indigenous Education, 43*(1), 52–57.	Australia
Barney, K., Shannon, C., & Nakata, M. (2014). Introduction: Exploring the scope of the Australian Indigenous studies learning and teaching network. *The Australian Journal of Indigenous Education, 43*(1), 1–7.	Australia
Biermann, S., & Townsend-Cross, M. (2008). Indigenous pedagogy as a force for change. *The Australian Journal of Indigenous Education, 37*(S1), 146–154.	Australia
Carey, M. (2015). The limits of cultural competence: An Indigenous studies perspective. *Higher Education Research & Development, 34*(5), 828–840.	Australia
Carlson, B., Berglund, J., Harris, M., & Poata-Smith, E. T. A. (2014). Four scholars speak to navigating the complexities of naming in Indigenous studies. *The Australian Journal of Indigenous Education, 43*(1), 58–72.	Australia
Champagne, D. (2007). In search of theory and method in American Indian studies. *American Indian Quarterly, 31*(3), 353–372.	United States

Cross-Townsend, M. (2011). Chapter Four: Indigenous Education and Indigenous Studies in the Australian Academy: Assimilationism, Critical Pedagogy, Dominant Culture Learners, and Indigenous Knowledges. *Counterpoints, 379,* 68–79. Australia

Everett, K. (2008). *Affecting change through assessment: Improving indigenous studies programs using engaging assessment.* ATN Assessment Conference 2008. (November 20–21, 2008, Adelaide). Australia

Fredericks, B. (2009). The epistemology that maintains white race privilege, power and control of Indigenous studies and Indigenous peoples' participation in universities. *Critical Race and Whiteness Studies, 5*(1), 1–12. Australia

Fry, M. R. (2018). *Sqwélqwel: A storybasket of the International Indigenous Studies Program at the University of Calgary.* (Unpublished master's thesis). University of Calgary, Calgary, AB. https://doi.org/10.11575/PRISM/5453 Canada

Herbert, J. (2010). Indigenous studies: Tool of empowerment within the academe. *The Australian Journal of Indigenous Education, 39*(S1), 23–31. Australia

Loyer, J., Vanderwerff, M., & Bowler, M. (2017). Supporting Indigenous Studies Programs through sustainable budget allocation. *Collection Management, 42*(3–4), 338–350. Canada

McGloin, C., & Carlson, B. L. (2013). Indigenous Studies and the politics of language. *Journal of University Teaching and Learning Practice, 10*(1), 1–10. Australia

McGloin, C., Marshall, A., & Adams, M. (2009). Leading the way: Indigenous knowledge and collaboration at the Woolyungah Indigenous centre. *Journal of University Teaching & Learning Practice, 6*(2), 1–15. Australia

McGloin, C. (2015). Listening to hear: Critical allies in Indigenous studies. *Australian Journal of Adult Learning, 55*(2), 267–282. Australia

Carey, M., & Prince, M. (2015). Designing an Australian Indigenous Studies curriculum for the twenty-first century: Nakata's 'cultural interface,' standpoints and working beyond binaries. *Higher Education Research & Development, 34*(2), 270–283. Australia

(continued)

(continued)

Article list for code source	Location
Nakata, M., Nakata, V., Keech, S., & Bolt, R. (2012). Decolonial goals and pedagogies for Indigenous studies. *Decolonization: Indigeneity, Education & Society, 1*(1), 120–140.	Australia
Nakata, M., Nakata, V., Keech, S., & Bolt, R. (2014). Rethinking majors in Australian Indigenous studies. *The Australian Journal of Indigenous Education, 43*(1), 8–20.	Australia
Nakata, M. (2007). The cultural interface. *The Australian Journal of Indigenous Education, 36*(S1), 7–14.	Australia
Olsen, T. A. (2017). Gender and/in indigenous methodologies: On trouble and harmony in indigenous studies. *Ethnicities, 17*(4), 509–525.	Norway
Rhea, Z. M., & Russell, L. (2012). The invisible hand of pedagogy in Australian Indigenous studies and Indigenous education. *The Australian Journal of Indigenous Education, 41*(1), 18–25.	Australia
Smith, L. T., Tuck, E., & Yang, K. W. (Eds.). (2018). *Indigenous and decolonizing studies in education: Mapping the long view.* Routledge.	Australia
Warrior, R. (2008). Organizing Native American and indigenous studies. *PMLA/Publications of the Modern Language Association of America, 123*(5), 1683–1691.	Canada

REFERENCES

Andersen, C. (2009). Critical Indigenous studies: From difference to density. *Cultural Studies Review, 15*(2), 80–100.

Andersen, C., & O'Brien, J. M. (Eds.). (2017). *Sources and methods in Indigenous studies.* Routledge.

Anonson, J., Huard, S., Kristoff, T., Clarke-Arnault, V., Wilson, E. V., & Walker, M. E. (2014). The role of elders in post-secondary educational institutes. *The Canadian Journal of Native Studies, 34*(2), 1–18.

Archibald, L. (2006). *Decolonization and healing: Indigenous experiences in the United States, New Zealand, Australia and Greenland.* Aboriginal Healing Foundation.

Assembly of First Nations. (n.d.). *About AFN: The Charter of the Assembly of First Nations.* https://www.afn.ca/about-afn/charter-of-the-assembly-of-first-nations/

Augustus, C. (2015). Knowledge liaisons: Negotiating multiple pedagogies in global Indigenous studies courses. *Canadian Journal of Higher Education, 45*(4), 1–17.

Barney, K. (2013). 'Taking your mob with you': Giving voice to the experiences of Indigenous Australian postgraduate students. *Higher Education Research & Development, 32*(4), 515–528.

Barney, K. (2014). A discussion with Sandy O'Sullivan about key issues for the Australian Indigenous studies learning and teaching network. *The Australian Journal of Indigenous Education, 43*(1), 52–57.

Barney, K., Shannon, C., & Nakata, M. (2014). Introduction: Exploring the scope of the Australian Indigenous studies learning and teaching network. *The Australian Journal of Indigenous Education, 43*(1), 1–7.

Barnhardt, R., & Kawagley, A. O. (2005). Indigenous knowledge systems and Alaska Native ways of knowing. *Anthropology and Education Quarterly, 36*(1), 8–23. https://doi.org/10.1525/aeq.2005.36.1.008

Battiste, M. (2017). *Decolonizing education: Nourishing the learning spirit.* UBC Press.

Battiste, M., Bell, L., & Findlay, L. M. (2002). Decolonizing education in Canadian universities: An interdisciplinary, international, Indigenous research project. *Canadian Journal of Native Education, 26*(2), 82–95.

Bell, D., & Vucetic, S. (2019). Brexit, CANZUK, and the legacy of empire. *The British Journal of Politics and International Relations, 21*(2), 367–382. https://doi.org/10.1177/1369148118819070

Black Hills State University. (2020). American Indian Studies. https://www.bhsu.edu/academics/math-social-sciences/american-indian-studies/#:~:text=The%20AIS%20Program%20at%20BHSU,Center%20for%20American%20Indian%20Studies

Boldt, M., & Long, J. A. (1984). Tribal traditions and European-Western political ideologies: The dilemma of Canada's Native Indians. *Canadian Journal of Political Science/Revue Canadienne de Science Politique, 17*(3), 537–553. https://doi:10.1017/S0008423900031905

Braddy, P. W., Meade, A. W., & Kroustalis, C. M. (2006). Organizational recruitment website effects on viewers' perceptions of organizational culture. *Journal of Business and Psychology, 20*(4), 525–543. https://doi.org/10.1007/s10869-005-9003-4

Bramley, D., Hebert, P., Jackson, R. T., & Chassin, M. (2004). Indigenous disparities in disease-specific mortality, a cross country comparison: New Zealand, Australia, Canada, and the United States. *New Zealand Medical Journal, 117*(1207), 1–16.

Brayboy, B. M. J. (2004). Hiding in the ivy: American Indian students and visibility in elite educational settings. *Harvard Educational Review, 74*(2), 125–152.

Carey, M., & Prince, M. (2015). Designing an Australian Indigenous studies curriculum for the twenty-first century: Nakata's 'cultural interface,' standpoints and working beyond binaries. *Higher Education Research & Development, 34*(2), 270–283.

Carleton University. (2020). Indigenous Studies. https://carleton.ca/sics/indigenous-studies/

Champagne, D. (2007). In search of theory and method in American Indian studies. *American Indian Quarterly, 31*(3), 353–372.

Charnley, S., Fischer, A. P., & Jones, E. T. (2007). Integrating traditional and local ecological knowledge into forest biodiversity conservation in the Pacific Northwest. *Forest Ecology and Management, 246*(1), 14–28. https://doi.org/10.1016/j.foreco.2007.03.047

Cohen, J. (1988). *Statistical power analysis for the behavioral sciences* (2nd ed.). Lawrence Erlbaum Associates.

Cooke, M., Mitrou, F., Lawrence, D., Guimond, E., & Beavon, D. (2007). Indigenous well-being in four countries: An application of the UNDP's human development Index to Indigenous peoples in Australia, Canada, New Zealand, and the United States. *BMC International Health and Human Rights, 7*(1), 1–11. https://doi.org/10.1186/1472-698X-7-9

Cornell, S. (2006). *Indigenous peoples, poverty and self-determination in Australia, New Zealand, Canada, and the United States* (Joint occasional papers on Native affairs). Udall Center for Studies in Public Policy and Harvard Project on American Indian Economic Development.

Corntassel, J. (2012). Re-envisioning resurgence: Indigenous pathways to decolonization and sustainable self-determination. *Decolonization: Indigeneity, Education and Society, 1*(1), 86–101.

Cross-Townsend, M. (2011). Indigenous education and Indigenous studies in the Australian academy: Assimilationism, critical pedagogy, dominant culture learners, and Indigenous knowledges. *Counterpoints, 379*, 68–79.

Day, A., Nakata, V., Nakata, M., & Martin, G. (2015). Indigenous students' persistence in higher education in Australia: Contextualising models of change from psychology to understand and aid students' practices at a cultural interface. *Higher Education Research and Development, 34*(3), 501–512. https://doi.org/10.1080/07294360.2014.973379

Drew, J. A., & Henne, A. P. (2006). Conservation biology and traditional ecological knowledge: Integrating academic disciplines for better conservation practice. *Ecology and Society, 11*(2), 1–9.

Fox, E. (2006). Indian education for all: A tribal college perspective. *Phi Delta Kappan, 88*(3), 208–212. https://doi.org/10.1177/003172170608800317

Fredericks, B. (2009). The epistemology that maintains White race privilege, power and control of Indigenous studies and Indigenous peoples' participation in universities. *Critical Race and Whiteness Studies, 5*(1), 1–12.

Fry, M. R. (2018). *Sqwélqwel: A Storybasket of the international Indigenous studies program at the University of Calgary* [Unpublished master's thesis]. University of Calgary. http://dx.doi.org/10.11575/PRISM/5453

Gagnon, C. A., & Berteaux, D. (2009). Integrating traditional ecological knowledge and ecological science: A question of scale. *Ecology and Society, 14*(2), 1–23.

Garcia, J., & Shirley, V. (2012). Performing decolonization: Lessons learned from Indigenous youth, teachers and leaders' engagement with critical Indigenous pedagogy. *Journal of Curriculum Theorizing, 28*(2), 76–91.

Gay, G. (1983). Multiethnic education: Historical developments and future prospects. *The Phi Delta Kappan, 64*(8), 560–563.

Giacon, J., & Simpson, J. (2012). Teaching Indigenous languages at universities. In C. Travis, J. Hajek, C. Nettlebeck, E. Beckmann, & A. Lloyd-Smith (Eds.), *The next step: Selected proceedings of the Inaugural LCNAU Colloquium* (pp. 61–74). LCNAU.

Government Accountability Office. (2018). *Tribal broadband: FCC's data overstate access, and Tribes face barriers accessing funding*. Testimony before the Committee on Indian Affairs, U.S. Senate. GAO-19-134T. https://www.gao.gov/products/gao-19-134t

Gray, J., & Beresford, Q. (2008). A "formidable challenge": Australia's quest for equity in Indigenous education. *Australian Journal of Education, 52*(2), 197–223. https://doi.org/10.1177/000494410805200207

Hunter, E., & Harvey, D. (2002). Indigenous suicide in Australia, New Zealand, Canada, and the United States. *Emergency Medicine, 14*(1), 14–23. https://doi.org/10.1046/j.1442-2026.2002.00281.x

Huntington, H. P. (2000). Using traditional ecological knowledge in science: Methods and applications. *Ecological Applications, 10*(5), 1270–1274. Error! Hyperlink reference not valid.https://doi.org/10.1890/1051-0761(2000)010[1270:UTEKIS]2.0.CO;2

Huntington, H. P. (2002). Can traditional ecological knowledge and wilderness benefit one another? In A. E. Watson, L. Alessa, & J. Sproull (Eds.), *Wilderness in the Circumpolar North: Searching for compatibility in traditional, ecotourism, and ecological values* (pp. 64–68). U.S. Department of Agriculture, Forest Service, Rocky Mountain Research Station.

Jackson, A. P., Smith, S. A., & Hill, C. L. (2003). Academic persistence among Native American college students. *Journal of College Student Development, 44*(4), 548–565.

John, O. P., & Benet-Martinez, V. (2000). Measurement: Reliability, construct validation, and scale construction. In H. T. Reis & C. M. Judd (Eds.), *Handbook of research methods in social and personality psychology* (pp. 339–369). Cambridge University Press.

Jonsen, K., Point, S., Kelan, E. K., & Grieble, A. (2021). Diversity and inclusion branding: a five-country comparison of corporate websites. *The International Journal of Human Resource Management, 32*(3), 616–649. https//:doi.org/10.1080/09585192.2018.1496125

Kovach, M. (2009). *Indigenous methodologies: Characteristics, conversations, and contexts.* University of Toronto Press.

Krippendorff, K. (1989). Content analysis. In E. Barnouw, G. Gerbner, W. Schramm, T. L. Worth, & L. Gross (Eds.), *International encyclopedia of communication,* Vol. 1 (pp. 403–407). Oxford University Press.

Krippendorff, K. (2018). *Content analysis: An introduction to its methodology.* SAGE.

Loyer, J., Vanderwerff, M., & Bowler, M. (2017). Supporting Indigenous studies programs through sustainable budget allocation. *Collection Management, 42*(3–4), 338–350.

Martin, G., Nakata, V., Nakata, M., & Day, A. (2017). Promoting the persistence of Indigenous students through teaching at the cultural interface. *Studies in Higher Education, 42*(7), 1158–1173. https://doi.org/10.1080/03075079.2015.1083001

McGloin, C., & Carlson, B. L. (2013). Indigenous Studies and the politics of language. *Journal of University Teaching and Learning Practice, 10*(1), 1–10.

McHugh, M. L. (2012). Interrater reliability: The kappa statistic. *Biochemia Medica, 22*(3), 276–282.

McIntyre, C., Harris, M. G., Baxter, A. J., Leske, S., Diminic, S., Gone, J. P., Hunter, E., & Whiteford, H. (2017). Assessing service use for mental health by Indigenous populations in Australia, Canada, New Zealand, and the United States of America: A rapid review of population surveys. *Health Research Policy and Systems, 15*(67), 1–17. https://doi.org/10.1186/s12961-017-0233-5

Morris, T.L., & Meinrath, S.D. (2009). New media, technology and Internet use in Indian country: Quantitative and qualitative analyses. Washington, DC: New America Foundation. https://ils.unc.edu/courses/2016_fall/inls539_001/BackupPDFs/NewMediaTechnologyAndInternetUseInIndianCountry.pdf

Murry, A. T., Barnabe, C., Foster, S., Taylor, A. S., Atay, E. J., Henderson, R., & Crowshoe, L. (2021). Indigenous mentorship in the health sciences: Actions and approaches of mentors. *Teaching and Learning in Medicine*, 1–11. https://doi.org/10.1080/10401334.2021.1912610

Murry, A. T., & James, K. (2021). Reconciliation and industrial–organizational psychology in Canada. *Canadian Journal of Behavioural Science/Revue canadienne des sciences du comportement, 53*(2), 114–124. https://doi.org/10.1037/cbs0000237

Murry, A., James, K., & Drown, D. (2013). From pictures to numbers: Vision mapping and sustainability collaboration between Native American community members and mainstream scientists. *American Indian Culture and Research Journal, 37*(4), 1–24.

Murry, A. T., & Wiley, J. (2017). Barriers and solutions: Direction for organizations that serve Native American parents of children in special education. *Journal of American Indian Education, 56*(3), 3–33. https://doi.org/10.5749/jamerindieduc.56.3.0003

Nakata, M. (2003). Indigenous knowledge and the cultural interface: Underlying issues at the intersection of knowledge and information systems. In A. Hickling-Hudson, J. Mathews, & A. Woods (Eds.), *Disrupting preconceptions: Postcolonialism and education* (pp. 19–38). Post Pressed. https://doi.org/10.1177/034003520202800513

Nakata, M. (2004). Ongoing conversations about Aboriginal and Torres Strait Islander research agendas and directions. *The Australian Journal of Indigenous Education, 33*, 1–6. http://hdl.handle.net/10453/9852

Nakata, M. (2006). Australian Indigenous studies: A question of discipline. *The Australian Journal of Anthropology, 17*(3), 265–275. https://doi.org/10.1111/j.1835-9310.2006.tb00063.x

Nakata, M. (2011). Pathways for Indigenous education in the Australian curriculum framework. *The Australian Journal of Indigenous Education, 40*, 1–8. https://doi.org/10.1375/ajie.40.1

Nakata, M. (2013). The Rights and blights of the politics in Indigenous higher education. *Anthropological Forum, 23*(3), 289–303. https://doi.org/10.1080/00664677.2013.803457

Nakata, M., Nakata, V., Keech, S., & Bolt, R. (2012). Decolonial goals and pedagogies for Indigenous studies. *Decolonization: Indigeneity, Education and Society, 1*(1), 120–140.

Nakata, M., Nakata, V., Keech, S., & Bolt, R. (2014). Rethinking majors in Australian Indigenous studies. *The Australian Journal of Indigenous Education, 43*(1), 8–20. https://doi.org/10.1017/jie.2014.3

National Congress of American Indians. (n.d.). *Mission and History*. https://www
.ncai.org/about-ncai/mission-history

Pavel, M. D., Inglebret, E., & Banks, S. R. (2009). Tribal colleges and universities in an era of dynamic development. *Peabody Journal of Education, 76*(1), 50–72. https://doi.org/10.1207/S15327930PJE7601_04

Pelletier, J., & Gercken, B. (2006). The "old ways" as new methods: Decolonizing and Native values in academia. *Studies in the Humanities, 33*(2), 245–264.

Ray, L. (2012). Deciphering the "Indigenous" in Indigenous methodologies. *Alternative: An International Journal of Indigenous Peoples, 8*(1), 85–98. https://doi .org/10.1177/117718011200800107

Rehyner, J., & Singh, N. K. (2010). Cultural genocide in Australia, Canada, New Zealand, and the United States. *Indigenous Policy Journal, 21*(4), 1–26.

Rushing, S. C., & Stephens, D. (2011). Use of media technologies by Native American teens and young adults in the Pacific Northwest: Exploring their utility for designing culturally appropriate technology-based health interventions. *The Journal of Primary Prevention, 32*, 135–145. https://doi.org/10.1007 /s10935-011-0242-z

Showalter, E., Moghaddas, N., Vigil-Hayes, M., Zegura, E. W., & Belding, E. M. (2019, January). Indigenous internet: Nuances of Native American internet use. In *Proceedings of the Tenth International Conference on Information and Communication Technologies and Development* (pp. 1–4). Association for Computing Machinery. https://doi.org/10.1145/3287098.3287141

Simon Fraser University. (2020). *Indigenous Studies*. https://www.sfu.ca/indg .html

Simonds, V. W., & Christopher, S. (2013). Adapting Western research methods to Indigenous ways of knowing. *American Journal of Public Health, 103*(12), 2185–2192. https://doi.org/10.2105/AJPH.2012.301157

Smillie-Adjarkwa, C. (2005). *Is the internet a useful resource for Indigenous women living in remote communities in Canada, Australia and New Zealand to access health resources?* National Network for Aboriginal Mental Health Research.

Smith, L. T. (2012). *Decolonizing methodologies: Research and Indigenous peoples* (2nd ed.). Zed Books.

Smith, L. T., Tuck, E., & Yang, K. W. (Eds.). (2019). *Indigenous and decolonizing studies in education: Mapping the long view.* Routledge.

Smylie, J., Crengle, S., Freemantle, J., & Taualii, M. (2010). Indigenous birth outcomes in Australia, Canada, New Zealand, and the United States—An overview. *Canadian Institutes of Health Research, 4*, 7–17.

Steinman, E. W. (2015). Decolonization not inclusion: Indigenous resistance to American settler colonialism. *Sociology of Race and Ethnicity, 2*(2), 219–236. https://doi.org/10.1177/2332649215615889

Thaman, K. H. (2003). Decolonizing Pacific studies: Indigenous perspectives, knowledge, and wisdom in higher education. *The Contemporary Pacific, 15*(1), 1–17. https://doi.org/10.1353/cp.2003.0032

Truth and Reconciliation Commission of Canada, United Nations. University of Manitoba. (2015). *Truth and reconciliation: Calls to action.* https://www2.gov

.bc.ca/assets/gov/british-columbians-our-governments/indigenous-people
/aboriginal-peoples-documents/calls_to_action_english2.pdf

United Nations General Assembly (2007). *Declaration on the rights of Indigenous peoples. Paris.* https://www.un.org/development/desa/indigenouspeoples
/declaration-on-the-rights-of-indigenous-peoples.html

University of British Columbia (2020). *First Nations and Indigenous Studies.* https://
fnis.arts.ubc.ca/

University of Calgary. (n.d.a). *Indigenous Student Access Program.* https://www
.ucalgary.ca/student-services/writing-symbols/prospective-students/isap

University of Calgary. (n.d.b). Taylor Institute for Teaching and Learning. https://
taylorinstitute.ucalgary.ca/pure-awards

University of Calgary. (2017). *ii'taa'poh'to'p (a place to rejuvenate and re-energize during a journey). Together in a good way: A journey of transformation and renewal.* Retrieved January 5, 2022, from https://www.ucalgary.ca/live-uc-ucalgary-site
/sites/default/files/teams/136/Indigenous%20Strategy_Publication_digital
_Sep2019.pdf

University of Fraser Valley (2020). *Indigenous Studies.* https://www.ufv.ca/indi
genous-studies/

University of Waikato. (2020). *Maori and Indigenous Studies.* https://www.waikato
.ac.nz/study/campaigns/maori-and-indigenous-studies

Walter, B., & Andersen, C. (2016). *Indigenous statistics: A quantitative research methodology.* Routledge. https://doi.org/10.4324/9781315426570

Warrior, R. (2008). Organizing Native American and Indigenous studies. *PMLA/
Publications of the Modern Language Association of America, 123*(5), 1683–1691.

Wilson, S. (2008). *Research Is ceremony: Indigenous research methods.* Fernwood Publishing.

Contributor Information

The *Journal of American Indian Education* (*JAIE*) is a refereed journal publishing original scholarship about education issues of American Indians, Alaska Natives, Native Hawaiians, and Indigenous peoples worldwide, including First Nations, Māori, Aboriginal/Torres Strait Islander peoples, Indigenous peoples of Latin America, Africa, and others. *JAIE* strives to improve Indigenous education through empirical research; knowledge generation; and transmission to researchers, communities, and diverse educational settings.

JAIE encourages dialogues among researchers and practitioners through research-based articles elucidating current educational issues and innovations. *JAIE* also invites original scholarly essays advancing a point of view about an educational question or issue, when supported by cited research literature; original reviews of literature in underexplored areas; original expository manuscripts that develop or interpret a theory or issue; and Reports From the Field. Studies grounded in Indigenous research methodologies are especially encouraged.

Prepare manuscripts according to the most recent *Publication Manual of the American Psychological Association* (7th ed.) (http://www.apastyle.org/manual/index.aspx). Format manuscripts in Microsoft Word and blind for anonymous peer review; manuscripts not blinded or appropriately formatted will be returned. Authors must certify that the manuscript is not being considered by another publisher. All empirical studies must document: (1) the use of accepted ethical protocols for research with human subjects; and (2) site-specific approvals, including research and/or institutional review board approvals required by Native nations, tribes, or bands as well as schools and school districts, where appropriate. Please use the term most appropriate to the Indigenous group or people to whom the manuscript refers. *American Indian/Alaska Native, Native American, Native Hawaiian,* and *Indigenous* are acceptable terms when referring to Indigenous peoples of the United States. *JAIE* reviews only one manuscript at a time from an author (or co-author). If a manuscript is under review, the Editorial Team cannot accept another manuscript (either single authored or co-authored) until the first manuscript clears the review process.

All manuscripts must be submitted electronically to jaie@asu.edu. Submit: (1) double-spaced manuscript as one Word document (do not send a pdf), including the title and abstract (maximum 150 words); (2) biographical statement(s) for each author (50 words each), and contact information for each author, including author name, affiliation, email address, physical street address; and phone number. Do not include author name(s) on or in the manuscript.

Feature-length Manuscripts Original scholarly manuscripts should be double-spaced, 7,500–8000 words total, including endnotes, if any, and references.

Reports From the Field Original scholarly manuscripts providing descriptive, evaluative, and/or policy- oriented analyses of innovative education models and practices may be considered as "Reports From the Field." Reports should be up to 5,000 words, including endnotes, if any, and references. See the website and *JAIE* 49(3) for a fuller description of "Reports From the Field."

Indigenous Policy Forum Invited manuscripts. The *IPF* functions as a current conversational space and as important historical archive, featuring the voices and vision of Indigenous education policymakers, policy implementers, and activists.

Manuscripts will be considered throughout the year and, if accepted, will be published in any of the three issues at the direction of the editorial staff. There is no remuneration for *JAIE* contributors; authors will receive two free copies of the issue in which the manuscript is published. For more information see the *JAIE* website at http://jaie.asu.edu.